Forgotten Missourians Who Made History

Forgotten Missourians Who Made History

Missourians who made lasting contributions to our state and nation yet are largely forgotten by subsequent generations

Compiled and edited
by Jim Borwick and Brett Dufur

Written by
Jim Borwick, Brett Dufur, Joan Gilbert,
Margot Ford McMillen, Dorothy Heckmann Shrader,
William Taft and Pamela Watson

Illustrations by
Joe Fox

Pebble Publishing
Columbia, Missouri

Project support by Pebble Publishing staff:
Brett Dufur, Daisy Dufur, Pippa Letsky and Heather Starek.

ISBN 0-9646625-8-2 14.95

Pebble Publishing, P.O. Box 431, Columbia, MO 65205-0431
Phone: (573) 698-3903 Fax: (573) 698-3108
E-Mail: pebble@global-image.com

Printed by Ovid Bell Press, Fulton, Missouri, USA.

Dedicated to

You, who, like the people within these pages,

can take your inspiration and turn it into reality.

True merit is like a river; the deeper it gets the less noise it makes.

— Anonymous

Novinger Record, 1906

Acknowledgments

A special thanks go out to Jim, Joe, Margot, Pamela, Bill, Dorothy and Joan for helping to create this book. An additional note of praise goes to Pippa and Heather for riding the tumultuous wave of book publishing with me. To our friends, families and dogs, too, go the greatest thanks of all.

Other Books in the Show Me Missouri Series:

99 Fun Things to Do in Columbia and Boone County

A to Z Missouri: The Dictionary of Missouri Place Names

Best of Missouri Hands

Daytrip Missouri

Exploring Missouri Wine Country

Forgotten Missourians Who Made History

The Complete Katy Trail Guidebook

What's That? A Nature Guide to the Missouri River Valley

Wit & Wisdom of Missouri's Country Editors

Contents

Contents

Preface

These pages are filled with Missourians, largely forgotten by subsequent generations, who made lasting contributions to our state or nation. Since there are already many resources that include biographies of famous Missourians such as Harry Truman, we sought their counterparts who remain far from the limelight of history's pages. Here we sought to create a book celebrating the forgotten Missourians who made history. You may well know several of the people listed within, but I doubt you know all of them. All were important to the growth and construction of our state and nation, yet their deeds have been superceded by the countless others that have also forged ahead with inspiration and idealism.

As our cadre of authors dug deeper into the fabric of heritage, struggle and strife that came to be known as Missouri, many questions arose that were not easy to answer. First of all, just how forgotten did someone have to be to be included? We decided that indeed, no one here had been completely forgotten, since we required extensive research to write their biographies. Instead, Jim and I recruited the help of many other Missouri authors who are firmly rooted in the heritage of our state. A phone call and simple questioning was all it took to get a flood of outstanding individuals for inclusion in our book.

Author Dorothy Heckmann Shrader is the perfect example. Her love has always been the river. In fact, she's published several books dealing with the steamboat era on the Missouri River. As soon as my question was asked, she started into a barrage of amazing individuals whose fate has failed to survive the piling up of historical figures. Sure, her famous riverboating family is still well known around Hermann and other river towns, and her family is well known to river aficionados, but what about today's kids? Her family and their rich riverboating past was exactly the kind of Missouri family I had hoped to include.

As we would find an individual for possible inclusion, Jim and I would ask our friends and families, say, do you know so-and-so? The famous Missourians became obvious immediately, and the forgotten Missourians came in close behind.

We included a good number of forgotten Missourians who made history in this book, but this is by no means inclusive. There is no way an author could hope to list all Missourians who made a contribution — especially all of those that have been forgotten!

Our hope is that this book will bring interested readers closer to the roots of our state by highlighting some interesting — and often eccentric — Missourians of the past.

Interest definitely played a part in our selection of which folks to include. Too often, history books don't get read because they're boring! We wanted this book to be used, and to spur further investigation into our rich past. In making our selections, we often gave precedence to the more interesting and enlightening individuals.

Obviously, this work could encompass many volumes if we were to claim academic intentions. Instead, this book is a primer, an introduction to our past. We felt much like Thomas Hart Benton when he was given the chance to celebrate the true Missouri atop the Capitol's bare walls with his color and paint brush. He chose not to feature its famous sons, but rather the true pioneers and Americans whose diligence and perseverance made the state as strong as it is today. This is the same feeling that pervades these pages.

The following individuals were also chosen for their uniqueness of the age. Many of these people may not seem surprising, cutting edge or innovative today, but they were considered lunatic fringe visionaries then. Take Luella Owen, for example. Exploring caves, or spelunking, was just not the right thing for a young lady to be doing. The contents pages will give you a quick overview of the wide range of their past achievements.

Perhaps the most important commonality of the people highlighted within these pages is they had the courage to follow their dreams and ambitions despite many obstacles and much criticism from their peers. These stories are a subtle way to learn a little history and impart a larger lesson about following our dreams and hearts to achieve what may perhaps seem clear only within our inner selves. It is our hope that this volume will leave you with a lasting appreciation of the many characters and visions that came to weave the rich fabric of our state.

Brett Dufur
Editor and Publisher
Pebble Publishing
Rocheport, MO

Forgotten Missourians Who Made History

"his campaign slogan . . . 'Run, Dick. Dick can help you. Run, Dick, run.'"

Sterl Artley

Teaching America to Read:

One of the creators of the *Dick and Jane* series

Sterl Artley grew up loving to read, which led him to help create a series of books with a special place in the hearts of baby boomers and others who learned to read watching Dick and Jane and Sally go. Artley helped write the Basic Readers series (more commonly known as the *Dick and Jane* series), primer reading books popular in the late 1950s and 1960s.

Two of the more popular primers include *Fun with Our Friends* and *More Fun with Our Friends*. Their covers bring back immediate memories, making the books now a collectors' item.

"I had hundreds of them," Artley said. "I gave them away and gave them away and finally I gave all of mine away. I had to borrow these from my daughter."

Artley got involved in the Basic Readers writing project in the late 1920s through a colleague. Dr. W. S. Gray at the University of Chicago contacted Artley about writing some children's books for Scott Foresman Publishing, a major textbook publisher. Artley and Gray collaborated on three books: *We Three*, *What Next?* and *Tall Tales*. That got him started with Scott Foresman, Artley said.

Traveling back and forth to Chicago, Artley continued to work on the reading series project. Artley's role was to write the teachers' manuals.

"These were to be used for reading instruction," he said. "Accompanying these for the teacher was the guidebook that outlined for her the lesson plans for every day. That is what I did, planned what she was to do and, literally, what she was to say, what competencies she was to develop, what she was to review. It was all spelled out. I think they were used in most schools in the U.S."

Though Artley grew up in Williamsburg, Pennsylvania, he retired in Missouri. From learning to read at a rural school, where his sister, ten years older, was his first-grade teacher, Artley went on to help teach America to read. After completing his doctorate in psychology at Penn State, Artley and his wife, Dorothy, moved to Columbia, Missouri, where he accepted a position at Stephens College as professor of psychology.

After two years he went to work for the University of Missouri.

"I saw a need for a reading clinic or a child study clinic," Artley said. "We started that at the university." He also supervised teachers-in-training and taught linguistics and reading classes.

"So my whole life has been involved in the general field of reading, one way or the other," he said.

Artley taught at the university until his retirement in 1986. During that time he wrote professionally for teachers' magazines and gave workshops and lectures that took him all over the country. He said there weren't many states he hadn't been in by the time he finished, including Alaska.

Whatever happened to Dick, Jane, Sally and Spot? Well, . . . "They grew up like everybody else. Dick ran for the state legislature and won. Political analysts say he won for two reasons. One was all the support given him by people, now adults, who knew him in school. Second was his campaign slogan, which was 'Run, Dick. Dick can help you. Run, Dick, run!'"

After his wife died, Artley moved into the Tiger Kensington where he is the resident celebrity. Many seek him out, he said, to interview him about his famous connection.

"Somehow they run me down, find out where I am," he said. "I don't know how many copies of books I have autographed. Hundreds, it seems."

Artley likes the way they teach reading in Columbia these days, using trade books to support reading topics.

"I'm in favor of that," Artley said. "I want children to be involved with reading, lots of it. I want them to enjoy reading."

Artley figures people will wonder about the Basic Readers' gang of Dick, Jane, Sally, Puff and Spot.

"People ask, whatever happened to them?" Artley said. "They grew up like everybody else. Dick ran for the state legislature and won. Political analysts say he won for two reasons. One was all the support given him by people, now adults, who knew him in school. Second was his campaign slogan, which was 'Run, Dick. Dick can help you. Run, Dick, run!'"

Artley said Jane became liberated. "Jane was an advocate of women's rights," Artley said.

"She had an ad in the Sunday paper that said, 'Help Jane win equal rights for women. Help Jane get into athletes' locker rooms.' Sally was a primary teacher. She had a whole room full of youngsters. She said to them, 'Jump, children, jump. When I say jump, jump!'"

Artley even has a theory as to what happened to the animals.

"Puff, bless her heart, was the one that really made it big," Artley said. "With the help of Madison Avenue, you can see her now on TV advertising cat food." But Spot?

"Spot, well, Spot sort of went to the dogs. Without guidance of his friends, he sort of grew up too fast. As a result, you can see little Spots all over the place."

It's good to know what happened to Dick and Jane and the rest of them. As for Artley, well, he takes walks and assists students, keeps up with his busy family and has fun with his friends.

". . . mow the yard on Saturday and be president of the United States on Sunday . . ."

David Atchison
President for a Day

So what are you going to do this weekend?
"Oh, mow the yard on Saturday and be president of the United States on Sunday."

It's hard to imagine Atchison's words as he came to hold the government's most powerful position for a day.

Though the saying is true that political careers are made and broken in a day, no one has proven this saying more readily than David Atchison.

While in the U.S. Senate, Atchison was for a large part of his two terms its presiding officer. It was while serving as president *pro tem* of the Senate that he became acting president of the United States for one day — the only Missourian ever to hold this office.

This is how it happened: President Polk's term expired on March 3, 1849. The next day was Sunday, so the inauguration of the new president was set for Monday, March 5, 1849. Thus, by virtue of his office as president of the Senate, Atchison became the Acting President of the United States.

Obviously, Atchison's presidency is but a footnote to his larger political contribution as U.S. senator. As with many other great politicians from Missouri, in spite of his great wealth, Atchison was not an aristocrat but lived the life of a democrat by nature and by education. He considered himself one of the people and was always near to them.

After his retirement from the U.S. Senate, Senator Atchison was active in the Kansas-Missouri border troubles. He was regarded as the pro-slavery leader in these affairs and several times led forces on Kansas soil. During the Civil War he served with the Missouri troops in the southern cause and was present at several battles. He died at his home in Clinton County on January 26, 1886.

During his lifetime Atchison County, Missouri, was named in his honor, as was the city of Atchison, Kansas.

Senator David Atchison was a simple, plain man, who occupied a remarkably influential position as U.S. senator and one of the leaders of the pro-slavery forces in Missouri before the Civil War.

". . . the first black to ride in Madison Square Garden, by intervention of the Vanderbilt family"

Tom Bass
Expert Black Equestrian

Tom Bass was born a slave, but he was invited to Queen Victoria's Diamond Jubilee, three times rode in presidential inauguration parades and attracted celebrities to his hometown of Mexico, Missouri. Because of Bass's skill at training show horses, Buffalo Bill Cody, Theodore Roosevelt, W. T. Barnum, Will Rogers, William Jennings Bryan, William McKinley, William Howard Taft and Grover Cleveland all shopped in Mexico. He had check-writing privileges with most of the horse owners who employed him, so he could, the instant he came across it, buy anything that would be suitable for them; they trusted his judgment and his honesty. In order to be with Bass and learn what they could from him, even in segregationist times, whites of all ages traveled with him in Jim Crow seats and ate in black-run restaurants.

Some who have written about Tom Bass credit him with charting his course carefully. He put himself where he could have most contact with horsemen, at the Ringo Hotel in Mexico. This was the favorite meeting place of the many professional trainers, who gathered in the barns in those days and helped give Mexico the title of Saddle Horse Capital of the World.

Bass's descendants say that Tom's maternal grandfather was a coachman and was manager of his owner's carriage horses and taught his small grandson all he could, to ease his life as a slave. Possibly the grandfather had also given advice about how best to use his abilities in freedom. One story is that Bass got his start driving the Ringo hack, a vehicle that met the trains to carry passengers to the hotel. By making his hack and team look outstanding, Bass gained notice and the opportunity to work in some of Mexico's good training barns.

There, because he was young and because he was black, he was given the least pleasant and least interesting work to do, at times the most dangerous work, but he learned from everything he did and became especially adept at handling troublesome horses. This proved an impediment to his progress, because he was given the job of salvaging those who'd been ruined by ignorant or abusive owners. His ability to make most of these animals useful and saleable brought him more assignments of the same kind.

Some say that Bass got out of this pocket with a young horse who was being discarded because he had panicked in a thunderstorm and impaled himself on a rail fence. The animal, disfigured and wild, supposedly was given to Bass in the same way many useless things were tossed to servants. Next show season, however, the colt, with its mane trained to fall over its scarred neck and shoulder, was a prize winner. This has been called the turning point in Bass's life, but some insist that the disfigured colt came later, after Bass had already become established. What we do know is that, somehow, Tom Bass forced people to acknowledge how well he could exhibit a saddle horse, and owners began asking his employer to assign him theirs.

Bass's success was so great that color lines were stretched for him, though in general, blacks were banned from the show ring for many decades after slavery ended. Bass (who was half-white or maybe more) was permitted to ride almost everywhere. He was the first black to ride in Madison Square Garden, by intervention of the Vanderbilt family. His ability and personality were such that other trainers, instead of rejoicing if he had problems, closed ranks around him. Mexico trainer John Hook told of one show where Bass had been informed he couldn't exhibit, and he was packing up to go home.

"We left our horses standing and showed his," Hook said. "Being mad, I guess we did extra well, for he got every ribbon he had hoped for. We told everyone we'd do it again any time we needed to, and I never know of him being banned again."

In 1893, in Kansas City, Bass established his own training stable and spent a few years there, but then he returned to Mexico where he remained until his death in 1934. His barn was recently obtained by the Audrain County Historical Society for restoration.

Many animals who are now famous among saddle horse fanciers were trained or shown by Tom Bass. With a lovely gray mare named Miss Rex he defeated her sibling, the immortal Rex McDonald. He trained a remarkable high school and trick horse named Columbus, whom William Cody bought to ride in parades and show entrances. Gray Columbus went well with Cody's white costumes and they made a striking pair, but Bass never forgave Cody for leasing Columbus out to someone who let him die in a barn fire.

Hundreds of big name horses shared Bass's career, but the one he cared most about was a black mare named Belle Beach. After she won all that could be won as a five-gaited mare, Bass taught her tricks and dances, creating a repertoire exceeding that of any horse before or since. This was an unusually intelligent animal. Bass said of her, "She's got more sense than most people" and "She knows very well that she is beautiful. If she sees two people watching her, she puts on a show."

Bass and Belle Beach traveled all over the United States and into Canada, doing special performances at horse shows and other events, sometimes on theater stages.

Here's a typical description of the mare's work (remember, horse world reporters are notoriously flowery): "She spun as if driving herself into the ground. She whirled until her mane and tail were wrapped around her. She glided and floated and waltzed. She climbed the air. She did everything but fly."

Belle Beach lived to be 31, her last years as Bass's own possession, lovingly cared for. He lived only one year longer, but he said in his last interview that he would love to relive this life, that he felt very privileged to have been able to work with the most beautiful things on earth. The coming of cars, he said, was "emancipation for horses."

The Basses lived well during Tom's best years, but by the time of his death they were in much reduced circumstances. Bass had always been more interested in the individual animals than in the business side of his work. Unable to read when he first began, he married a former schoolteacher, Angie Jewell, who taught him what he most needed to know and relieved him of business correspondence and bookkeeping details.

One example of how Bass failed to accumulate riches is that, when he designed a bit that made controlling show horses much easier without causing them as much distress as most bits did, he never did get to patent it. Interested friends urged him to do so, but others got the profit from making and merchandizing it. And they still do: the Tom Bass bit appears in most of the catalogs used by show people.

The reading of condolences at Tom Bass's funeral was said to have taken almost two hours, and Will Rogers published a eulogy in his syndicated newspaper column that ended with a plea to St. Peter to let Tom Bass enter heaven on horseback.

Fishing for a medical breakthrough

William Beaumont
America's First Great Medical Scientist

No one had the stomach to test theories concerning human digestion until June 6, 1822, when Dr. William Beaumont was summoned from his crude frontier hospital at Fort Mackinac in the Michigan Territory. Arriving at the American Fur Company store, Beaumont found Alexis St. Martin, a Canadian trapper, with a shotgun hole blasted in his chest.

"I considered any attempt to save his life entirely useless," Beaumont wrote. However, not only did St. Martin survive the shotgun wound, he and Beaumont ended up conducting a series of medical experiments that made Beaumont's reputation as a pioneering physiologist.

Before then, two ideas had dominated debates over the stomach's role in human digestion. One theory pictured the stomach as a kind of fermenting vat, a cauldron of chemicals stoked by heat. A second theory suggested that digestion occurred mechanically — by grinding. Neither school had evidence to prove its claims, though not for lack of effort.

To test their beliefs, proponents of the chemical view experimented on buzzards, sheep, dogs, cats and even themselves. One Italian researcher, Lazzaro Spallanzani, fished for his own gastric juice by swallowing sponges tied to strings. Spallanzani was able to demonstrate that gastric juice would dissolve food outside his stomach. The chance to see if Spallanzani's findings held true within the stomach fell to Beaumont, an ambitious country doctor serving as a U.S. Army post surgeon on a remote island bustling with fur trade.

According to Reginald Horsman in *Frontier Doctor: William Beaumont, America's First Great Medical Scientist,* St. Martin's external wound healed. But despite repeated attempts to close it, a hole remained in his stomach wall. The experiments began at noon on August 1, 1825. Beaumont baited a string with food and lowered it into St. Martin's stomach cavity. Lunch for St. Martin that day consisted of seasoned a la mode beef, raw salted lean beef, raw salted fat pork, raw lean fresh beef, boiled corn beef, stale bread and raw cabbage. Beaumont removed the food at one, two and three o'clock to observe the rate of digestion.

The experiment ended at five o'clock. St. Martin felt weak, his stomach and head ached; the next day, he suffered indigestion. On August 7, a week after his first try, Beaumont siphoned an ounce of gastric juice from St. Martin's stomach. He placed the juice in a vial with a piece of corned beef as large as his pinky, corked the top, submerged the vial in a saucepan of water, heated it to 100° F and parked the vial in a sand bath to keep its temperature constant. At the same time, he slid a similar slab of corned beef into St. Martin's stomach, regularly removing it for observation. The experiment, repeated several times with different foods, did more to shed light on the role of gastric juice in human digestion than the years of theorizing that preceded it and provided the first physical evidence that simulated test-tube digestion closely resembles internal digestion.

In late 1825 Beaumont grudgingly suspended his experiments after St. Martin left Mackinac for Canada. Beaumont had hired the vulnerable, poverty-stricken trapper as a live-in handyman, an arrangement that provided St. Martin with an income and enabled Beaumont to experiment while closely monitoring his patient's condition. Understandably, St. Martin wished to resume his normal existence.

The experiments tested St. Martin's patience. Frequently, Beaumont removed food from the trapper's stomach during digestion to observe changes. St. Martin's suffering underwrote Beaumont's progress. The doctor's experiments at Prairie Du Chien helped confirm that digestion was a chemical process, in which gastric juice acted as a solvent.

Four years and many experiments later, Beaumont published the results of his 283 tests in *The Physiology of Digestion with Experiments on the Gastric Juice,* published in 1833. In it, Beaumont concluded that digestion is a chemical process and that gastric juice acts as a solvent.

His work won wide acceptance. Generally ignorant of the debates raging in Europe over the physiology of human digestion and aligned with no school or ideology, Beaumont was viewed as an objective observer and an honest reporter. His book — self-published and dedicated to his mentor, Surgeon General Lovell — eventually sold more than 3,000 copies in its first edition. It became a trusted source for medical students and opened new avenues of research.

Beaumont's peripatetic military career kept him moving. From 1825 through 1828 he served at Fort Niagara, Fort Howard and Fort Crawford. To continue his digestive experiments on St. Martin, Beaumont signed a contract with his subject and paid him an advance. But St. Martin disappeared into Canada, a foreign jurisdiction. Beaumont, writing Lovell, expressed the belief that St. Martin would eventually spend his advance and be "willing to recant his villainous obstinacy and ugliness, and then I shall be able to regain possession of him again, I have no doubt."

Meanwhile, Beaumont also attempted to persuade Congress to reimburse him the cost of his past experiments on St. Martin and to finance his future research. His proposal was shelved. In 1834, the army assigned Beaumont to Jefferson Barracks, ten miles from St. Louis, and then granted Beaumont's request to be stationed at the arsenal in St. Louis, which allowed him to establish a private practice. St. Louis was growing rapidly (its population doubled, then quadrupled, in the 1830s and 1840s), which kept Beaumont so busy in his lucrative private practice that he attempted to reject an offer in 1836 to become chair of surgery at St. Louis University's medical department. Though Beaumont made some desultory attempts to bring St. Martin to St. Louis to renew his experiments, his plans fell through.

Beaumont's thriving St. Louis practice was interrupted by ugly controversies. In 1840, Beaumont's medical treatment of Andrew Jackson Davis, owner of the *Missouri Argus*, brought him grief. Davis was attacked and caned on the head by William P. Darnes, a prominent local politician who had received unflattering coverage in the *Argus*. The assault fractured Davis's skull. A week after Beaumont operated, the patient died and Darnes was charged with third-degree manslaughter.

In Darnes's defense, his lawyer argued that it was not his client's caning but Beaumont's operation that had caused Davis's death. The defense called as expert witnesses several St. Louis physicians who criticized Beaumont's medical judgment, and the jury convicted Darnes on a lesser charge — fourth-degree manslaughter. Soon after the trial, Beaumont was elected president of the St. Louis Medical Society. After his term expired, he took no further part in the society's activities.

Embittered and increasingly deaf, Beaumont withdrew into the company of family and friends. He bought a big white frame house on 40 acres of land about a mile from the center of St. Louis, now bounded by Jefferson Avenue and Beaumont Street. After falling and hitting his head on ice-covered steps in March 1853, he died the following month from complications and was buried in Bellefontaine Cemetery in St. Louis.

**"social interaction and control . . .
constructive and aesthetic powers . . ."**

Susan Blow
Mother of America's Kindergarten

Blow's efforts to establish kindergartens in St. Louis grew out of her philosophical interests and her ambition. A serious, studious woman, the daughter of a wealthy St. Louis businessman and politician, she aspired, against her family's wishes, to become something other than a wife and a figure on the upper-class social circuit. Educated by private tutors at the family's Victorian-style house on 16 acres in Carondelet, a settlement five miles downriver from St. Louis, she developed a fondness for books that apparently survived two years at Ms. Haines's finishing school in New York City.

A follower of the German educational theorist Friedrich Froebel, Blow was among the first to bring Froebel's ideas on childhood learning into American public schools. Froebel, a philosophical idealist, believed that children developed best through supervised play. In the rigorous analytical spirit of philosophers, he classified play into two types. One type, games of imagination, required no materials. Through these games, children learned social cooperation and control. The other type of play involved materials such as yarn, paper and plant seeds. Through the use of these materials, children developed constructive and aesthetic powers.

In 1871, Blow returned to St. Louis from travels in Europe. Using her family connections, she contacted William T. Harris, St. Louis school superintendent, to discuss the possibility of starting a public-school kindergarten.

In August 1873, the St. Louis School Board approved her plan for a kindergarten. In September, the kindergarten, housed in Room 4 at Des Peres School on Michigan Avenue in St. Louis, opened its doors for 42 students. Blow dressed the drab classroom in bright colors, added floral touches and displayed the children's art on the bulletin boards. Low communal tables freed kindergartners from imprisonment behind individual desks. Blow organized the planting of a children's garden on the south side of the school, and the teachers kept precise records of the seeds' growth, from germination through maturity.

The kindergarten took root. The school board considered the first year's experiment a success; in its annual report the board expressed surprise at the rapidity of the children's progress in learning to draw, fold and model, and in recognizing forms, shapes and numbers. "It would seem as though," the board wrote, "Froebel had especially in view, the education of a race of industrious and useful people." During the next two years, the St. Louis public schools added two more kindergartens. Harris and Blow claimed that most of the kindergarten graduates entered first grade academically and socially more developed than the children who entered first grade without prior schooling.

St. Louis's kindergarten was the first of its kind, receiving national attention.

St. Louis's kindergarten experiment received national attention. In 1876, at the Centennial Exposition in Philadelphia, the city's kindergarten exhibit won top honors. Blow opened a training school for kindergarten teachers where she expounded on Froebel's theories. Her pupils went on to become leaders of the U.S. kindergarten movement.

Blow's affiliation with the St. Louis public school kindergartens all but ended in 1877. Her health deteriorated; to recuperate, she moved to Cazenovia, New York, and spent the final period of her life writing books, and lecturing on kindergarten and other subjects at Columbia University Teachers College in New York. She also served on the committee of the International Kindergarten Union. The Mother of Kindergarten died at Avon, New York, on March 26, 1916, of heart failure.

J. W. "Blind" Boone
Missouri's Musical Prodigy

Years before Texas-born Scott Joplin settled in Sedalia and published the *Maple Leaf Rag,* one of Missouri's native sons was traveling the world performing a mixture of classical music and his own compositions based on African folk tunes. He was called "Blind" Boone.

John William Boone, the son of a former slave, was born on May 14, 1864, in Miami, Missouri, to Rachel Boone, the cook for a Union troop based there. Her last name, as was often the case with slaves, was the name of her former owners, descendants of Daniel Boone. Whether John William was born blind is unknown, but it is recorded that when he was six months old, he was diagnosed with "brain fever," probably a form of encephalitis or meningitis. Doctors decided to remove his eyes, to release pressure on his brain and thus save his life. From then on he was known as "Blind Willie."

Willie soon showed a remarkable musical talent, happily banging on pots and pans with a rhythm unusual for a three-year-old. It wasn't long before Willie met his first piano, and neither he nor the piano were ever the same again.

After the war, Rachel and Willie moved to Warrensburg where Rachel worked as a maid in several large homes. Willie soon showed a remarkable musical talent, happily banging on pots and pans with a rhythm unusual for a three-year-old. It wasn't long before Willie met his first piano, and neither he nor the piano were ever the same again.

When Willie was eight, Rachel married widower Harrison Hendrix who had five children of his own. The little boy was delighted to be part of this large, boisterous family and quickly made friends with his new brothers and sisters. He loved Sunday church with its music and singing, and his talent grew, expressed first with a tin whistle and later with a harmonica. He organized his friends into a tin whistle band and was often invited to perform in private homes and at picnics. He was extremely bright and had the remarkable ability to memorize anything, including music, voices, even the feel of a handshake.

By age nine, Willie was well known around Warrensburg, and town citizens arranged for him to attend the St. Louis School for the Blind to learn a trade. Willie was not a great student and grew bored with the monotony of lessons. What he wanted to do was play music — any kind of music.

Willie loved to sneak into the practice room and listen to the students play. He soon made friends with Enoch Donley, one of the advanced pupils in the senior class, who saw Willie's potential and agreed to teach him to play. Donley wanted Willie to do it the hard way, through practice and repetition, but Willie could hear a piece played one time and copy it by feel and sound. He immersed himself in the classics and memorized the entire piano repertoire of Franz Liszt. By the end of his first year at school, Willie was able to perform a recital, to the amazement of the music professor.

Willie's second year at school was very different. Donley had graduated, and Willie was unable to keep his mind on anything but music. He began sneaking out at night to go listen to the black piano players in the taverns and honkytonks in town. He was eventually dismissed from school and in his early teens began performing with his harmonica on the streets of St. Louis. He was soon at the mercy of unscrupulous organizers and agents who had him barnstorming the state, often on foot, performing at fairs and in taverns. It wasn't until Columbia businessman John Lange Jr. heard him play and offered to manage his career that Willie's fortunes took a turn for the better.

Lange saw to it that Willie received some formal musical education. Billing him as "Blind" Boone, Lange arranged his first concert in Columbia, Missouri, in 1880 and from there the pair traveled all over the world. "Blind" Boone played in the gilded concert halls of Europe before monarchs and artists alike. Later in his career, one newspaper reported that the Russian composer Rachmaninoff declared Boone to be one of the "greatest talents of the day."

Boone played classical pieces and the new "ragtime" along with compositions of his own, which combined the two as well as gospel and African folk music. He described his programming of popular music along with the classics as "putting the cookies on the lower shelf so everyone can get at them." Many of his compositions were inspired by events and circumstances around him. One of his greatest rags, the *Marshfield Tornado,* was composed after hearing of the devastation caused by that event. In it he re-created musically the sounds of a great tornado, including church bells, thunder and the dripping of rain.

His first published work was a waltz, *Cleo* (1878). A hymn, *Where Shall We Go When the Great Day Comes?* (1894) was written in the baroque style of Handel or Bach, whereas *Sparks* (1894) was a quick-time musical vignette in 2/4 tempo. His *Blind Boone's Southern Rag Medleys* Nos 1 and 2, published in 1908-1909 at the height of the ragtime craze, became very popular.

Many of his compositions were never written down and are therefore lost to us today. He did, however, record a number of piano rolls, signing a five-year contract in 1912 with Q.R.S. Company of Chicago, still the leading piano roll manufacturer. Unfortunately, the *Marshfield Tornado* was neither published nor recorded, as Boone claimed he wanted to reserve this masterpiece for his own use, so we can only imagine what Boone's listeners heard as he pounded out the sounds of thunder and lightening.

Boone was tough on pianos. He loved to pound out a rag and in his early years ruined many a piano. During his 47-year career he had several pianos specially made for him by the Chickering Piano Company, the last of which was a nine-foot concert grand with a solid oak case, strung in England in 1891. This piano can be seen today in the Walters Boone County Historical Museum in Columbia, Missouri.

In 1889, Boone married Lange's sister, Eugenia, and the couple built a ten-room residence at 10 North Fourth Street in Columbia. He continued to play all over the world until Lange's death in 1919, when he lost enthusiasm for his music and his life onstage ended. "Blind" Boone died in Warrensburg in 1927 while visiting relatives and is buried alongside his beloved Eugenia in the Columbia Cemetery.

"dismounting a bit stiffly . . . adjusting his eye glasses"

Nathan Boone
The Other Boone, Pioneer and Scout

If Daniel Boone hadn't been so famous, his fifth son, Nathan, probably would be one of Missouri's best-remembered pioneers. Nathan actually accomplished much more than his father did, and much more that mattered. He was among those who framed our state's first constitution, and he surveyed the first road that went all the way across Missouri. He surveyed the border between Iowa and Missouri and traveled in many states to do other surveying. He served as military governor of New Mexico and as commander of the famous Fort Gibson, which was then Indian territory and today lies in Oklahoma. He fought in the Black Hawk War and the War of 1812, at one time riding with Zachary Taylor.

Many who touched lives with Nathaniel Boone became famous. Several were with him on a five-week excursion made in the heat of summer in 1834 to exchange prisoners and to try and make an impression with Western Indian tribes that refused to negotiate with the whites.

Present were Lt. Jefferson Davis, who would become the president of the Confederacy; Jesse Chisholm, guide interpreter for whom a famous trail would be named; George Catlin, whose sketches and paintings of the West are still treasured today; and Lt. Stephen W. Kearney, who distinguished himself in several wars.

They were commanded by Gen. Henry Leavenworth, who died in the heat, and then by Col. Henry Dodge. The party — made up of hundreds of soldiers, mounted and on foot, and four parties of mounted Indians of tribes friendly to the whites — was the largest military expedition ever made into Indian Territory.

Boone, a captain then, commanded one of nine companies of dragoons participating, but he may have been along partly for his guiding skills. He had led Gen. William Clark and his troops to the site selected for Fort Osage. Though he was 53 years old in the year of the Lewis and Clark expedition, he was much respected for his tracking ability and instinctive sense of direction and place.

One touching memory from a soldier who served under Boone was the picture of a little man, more than a little portly (like his father, Nathan was below average height), dismounting a bit stiffly, adjusting his eye glasses and kneeling on the trail to peer at signs only he could see. He would then arise and with casual confidence direct great columns of soldiers to follow a particular route.

Boone was noted also for his negotiating power with Indians, and this may have been another reason for his presence. Though several members of his extended family and two of his own brothers had been killed by Indians, Nathan Boone had a respectful understanding for native people that enabled him to gain their goodwill. Quaker heritage may have figured here, for the adventuresome Boones had been of this faith for at least two generations. When praised as a "wonderful man who killed a lot of Indians," Daniel Boone made a typically Quaker response: "I don't see what killing people has to do with being wonderful." He said he had killed only a few people of any color, just those who threatened his life or someone else's.

Regardless of Nathan Boone's role, all who went on that trip were brave, for they didn't know what they were going into. Tribes assembling at the northern fork of the Red River (western Oklahoma or northern Texas) were Kiowas, Comanches, Picts, Pawnees and Wacos. Boone and his companions knew they might be met by an army big enough to wipe them out, and they were. About 2,000 armed and mounted warriors confronted them, but somehow prisoners were exchanged and cordiality established. At the end of the visit, many Western Indians went back east with the party, and it's said they went back singing — sharing tribal songs, listening to songs of the Eastern Indians and the whites.

Boone was beloved of his troops, who said he was like "an old daddy" to them all, always concerned about their well-being, always trying to take the least dangerous course. He was apparently equally responsible to his own family, providing well, though he was away from them a great deal. One of his daughters wrote of the excitement when he came home after being absent for several months. His money belt would be heavy with the gold coins he had earned and he would dump these out on the bed or the rug for the children to count and play with.

Nathan Boone's marriage is probably as romantic as anything any novelist could conceive. When his family moved to Missouri from Virginia in 1799, Nathan, aged 18, was to help his brother Morgan bring the women of the family and the household goods by boat. Two days out, with Morgan's knowledge and agreement, he cast aside this duty and went back to the border of Ohio, where lived a 16-year-old girl named Olive Van Bibber. En route, he got a marriage license, and less than a week later the wedding was over and the young couple had started off to find the Boone family. Each rode a horse, and another horse carried belongings. In old age, Olive wrote of their trip, sleeping with feet to the campfire every night, as autumn deepened. The great undertaking of their trip was to cross the Missouri River near St. Charles. "My husband rowed the skiff loaded with our things while I steered and held the reins of the three horses swimming behind us," Olive wrote.

She bore 14 children to Nathan, 11 girls and 3 boys. Most of them grew up on 680 acres of fine land on the Femme Osage, which Nathan obtained at the age of 22. The price, according to the deed, was "a horse, a bridle and a saddle." There Nathan and his father and others built a lovely three-story house with granite from the property. It was seven years in the building because of Nathan's frequent absences, but the house is still beautiful and sound. It has the contrasting features of a ballroom on the third floor and shutters with gun ports inside the windows on the ground floor, in case Indians attacked.

At times, Nathan's parents lived with the growing family in this house, and it was there that Daniel Boone died in 1820. The younger Boones lost their home in 1836 because Nathan had signed a note for a friend who reneged. He then took his family, the youngest child ten years old, to some lovely land he had spotted much earlier while surveying. It was 1,200 acres abutting what are now the city limits of the town Ash Grove in Greene County, Missouri.

There he built a house luxurious for the time, a spacious double-log cabin with high ceilings, carpets and wallpaper. Boone had little time to enjoy this place and its peaceful surroundings, for he remained in military service until he was 72. Three years later, in 1856, he was dead, leaving an estate of $25,000, a fortune at the time. In only two more years, Olive followed her husband to rest quietly in a small family cemetery with a few of their grandchildren and other relatives.

In the Ash Grove area, Nathan Boone is anything but forgotten. Descendants still living there hold a Boone family rendezvous each October, which is open to the public and offers many pleasures to those who are interested in the family and in Missouri's history. The house is on the National Registry of Historic Places, and though it is not restored yet, it will be. At present, bus tours take people to visit the Boone cemetery and to see the work going on in the grounds to locate sites of outbuildings and slave quarters.

Pressing news and pressing times
for the “Father of Missouri Journalism”

Joseph Charless

Bringing the Free Press to Missouri

In St. Louis on July 12, 1808, the state's first newspaper arrived, the *Missouri Gazette*. Edited by Joseph Charless, a transplanted Irishman, the *Gazette* recorded the history of that area before Missouri officially became a state. Charless became known as the "Father of Missouri Journalism."

And since the beginning of the printed word, a historical record of Missouri has been recorded in the thousands of newspapers that followed. As years followed, publishers were to organize into the Missouri Press Association, and eventually one of the most complete files of these publications was assembled and microfilmed at the State Historical Society in Columbia, providing primary sources for historians, scholars, students, genealogists and others to study historical events and personalities.

The beginning of newspapering in Missouri was typical of that encountered in other states. Charless reached St. Louis in 1808, with his Ramage hand-operated press, some type and some paper. The press was mostly made of wood. The printing office was a log cabin. A typical printer could store all of his necessary equipment in a wagon, so he could move from place to place, seeking to strike it rich in some new territory. Few ever did, however. Apprentices were difficult to find, especially any young man who would remain with a printer long enough to learn the trade.

St. Louis was an appropriate locality for Charless to establish his operations. It was a river city, attracting immigrants from the East as well as from the South. And it was the gateway to the West. It was a frontier community, luring settlers from many states.

Pioneer newspapermen depended on job printing to survive, so it is no wonder that Charless first printed the laws for the Upper Louisiana territory before he established the *Missouri Gazette*. Charless received an advance of $225 for the printing of these laws and used the funds to purchase supplies. After starting the newspaper, Charless found it necessary to depend on a variety of businesses to make ends meet. It is doubtful if this newspaper, or many of those that followed, could have survived on circulation and advertising revenues alone.

Charless sought to provide readers with all of the available news. In his days "news" had a different meaning than today. Some of his stories had occurred months before. And, as today, the postal service was often blamed for the delay, since exchange papers were delayed by storms, floods and other hazards of nature that prevented the mails from coming through on a regular basis.

Still, what readers found in the paper would be new to them — at least, they had not known about these events before. And editors had no great inclination to be entirely neutral in what they selected to print from other publications or what they expressed in their own writings. As communities became crowded, these editors moved westward, seeking greater opportunities.

Thus Charless was as typical as a typical editor could be. He had come from Ireland by way of France to the eastern coast of America. He had attempted to publish newspapers in Pennsylvania and Kentucky communities and had failed. He had known Benjamin Franklin, Alexander Hamilton, Henry Clay and others. And like Franklin, Charless considered himself a printer, not an editor.

It was the practice for these printers to issue a prospectus, informing the public about their plans for a newspaper and its contents. These wordy predictions were then copied in other newspapers about the nation, serving as advertising messages. Charless's prospectus was typical, as these opening paragraphs reveal:

> "It is self evident that in every country where the rays of the Press are not clouded by despotic power, that the people have arrived to the highest grade of civilization, there science holds her head erect and bids her sons to call into action those talents which lie in a good and inviting civilization. The inviolation of the Press is co-existent with the liberties of the people, they live or die together, it is the vestal fire upon the preservation of which, the fate of nations depends; and the most pure hands officiating for the whole community, should be incessantly employed in keeping it alive.
>
> "It is now proposed to establish a Weekly Newspaper, to be published by subscriptions at St. Louis, to be called the:
>
> MISSOURI GAZETTE AND LOUISIANA ADVERTISER:
> BY JOSEPH CHARLESS"

It was to appear weekly, on "handsome type and paper" and the "day of publication will be regulated by the arrival of the Mail." Such a situation was to continue for many decades; editors depended on other newspapers for much of their material and thus quotes were printed and reprinted across the nation. Unfortunately, seldom did the author receive any credit for his creations.

Charless asked hopefully for payment in advance. Seldom did readers pay in advance, however. Too often the newspaper failed to survive long enough for the subscriber to get his money's worth. Charless claimed that $1,200 was owed him by subscribers after his first two years.

What was the "news"? Much of it was political in nature, often used in accordance with the political leanings of the editor. There was crime news, as well, the "criminals" then being the Indians. Editors did not consider any restrictions on what to print. For example, Charless stood for liberty of the press, so much so that his zeal to promote that liberty, and what he thought was just and right, sometimes led him to bend the truth. His feelings toward Indians and Englishmen often became apparent to readers, in the ways he might "bend the truth."

Newspapers spread across the state, going to Franklin where the *Missouri Intelligencer and Boon's Lick Advertiser* began in 1819. By the mid-1830s, newspapers had reached Ste. Genevieve, Palmyra, Boonville, Jefferson City, Cape Girardeau, Fayette, Independence, Bowling Green, Columbia and Liberty. The majority of these communities were on rivers.

It was an era when the editor and his readers knew each other; they were friends and neighbors, sharing their thoughts about the community and its needs. The editors were publishing a product that readers depended on for information about the area, the people, churches, schools, community projects and the like. In the midst of much factual information, they could enjoy original pithy comments to lighten the day. Through the years, however, as the emphasis shifted from the personal journalism approach to more objective reporting, such opinionated items tended to pass by the wayside.

Campaign papers appeared in these early decades as well, disappearing after the elections. And like the people in Missouri, the state newspapers split in their support of the North or the South during the Civil War. Newspaper offices were occasionally raided by the enemy, with the type melted into bullets. On occasions the other equipment would be thrown into the river or destroyed. One editor buried his equipment in his backyard before going to war.

Following this conflict, the editors tended to come together for their mutual interest. In sections of the state, editors and publishers associations were founded. On May 16, 1867, the Missouri Press Association was established and continues today to represent the state's newspapers. Eventually, this group helped establish the State Historical Society of Missouri in 1898 and the University of Missouri School of Journalism in 1908.

"the first home south of the Missouri River"

Hannah Cole
A Pioneer Mother

The remarkable adventures of early American explorers are well known. They were a colorful, boastful lot who caught the eye of the day's writers. We know less about the people who followed. These pioneers claimed a piece of ground, cleared it, raised families and tried to preserve a little of the art of civilization. It is impossible for us today to understand their endurance in the face of hardship, hunger and loneliness.

The Cole brothers from Virginia were cousins of the explorer Daniel Boone. The Boones had found a salt spring in present-day Howard County and were distilling salt and shipping it to St. Louis. Lured by news of the Boones' success, the Coles decided to move. By settling near the Boonslick Trail and the spring, the Cole men could help out at the saltworks while the women and children tended the farms.

Stephen and William Cole and their wives and children left St. Louis in 1810, with horses, wagons and provisions. The date of their departure is unknown, but they probably left in October or November, hoping to take advantage of the good fur-hunting season in winter. And they probably took enough provisions to outlast the cold, knowing that after the weather broke, they could survive on the area's abundant game. They were good hunters, all of them — men, women and children.

With some other families, the Coles made a temporary settlement at Loutre Island, near present-day Hermann. There, Indians stole seven of the horses. The men gave chase and William Cole was killed. His wife, Hannah, was now a widow with nine children: Jennie, Mattie, Kykie, Nellie, James, Holbert, Stephen, William and Samuel. Samuel was the youngest at about age nine.

We wish today that we had a record of Hannah's thoughts. A diary or letters home. What was going through her mind? Probably, the decision to go on was easily made. Pioneer parents of the time had great faith in their chance for success in the wilderness and many wanted only to live long enough to see their children settled on farms.

Was she tempted to turn back?

If she had, the younger children would have been taken from her and apprenticed to masters. As a woman, she would have been dependent on relatives. By continuing on, she had a chance of success. The children, some of them full-grown teenagers, had been raised in the frontier tradition. Although they had little, if any, formal education, they could survive on the gifts of nature. They were accustomed to hard work and danger.

The families left Loutre Island in December. Hannah's two surviving horses pulled a wagon with provisions. Their one milk cow walked ahead of them. After traveling 100 miles, they decided to cross the Missouri River. Later, as an adult, Samuel recalled: "We halted our team about where Old Franklin was afterwards built and came over the river in a pirogue, leaving our wagon on the other side and swimming our team. After arriving on this side we continued our journey for about a mile east of the present town of Boonville. . . . The river continued to be so full of ice, and was so swift, that we could not return to the opposite shore for eleven days."

In the bitter cold, the families huddled together under branches and animal skins. For eleven days, they survived on acorns, slippery elm bark and one wild turkey. When the weather finally broke, they returned for the wagon. Samuel remembered: "As soon as the ice had somewhat disappeared, we got in to the pirogue and recrossed, but the current and ice carried us two miles below before we could make a landing. After doing this we slowly worked our way up on the other side, reaching a point where we had left our wagon with some difficulty. We took the wagon apart (the boat not being large enough to carry it any other way) and came back."

In the spring, the families built two cabins on the river bluff about a mile apart. They cleared land and put in a small crop of corn. They fed and clothed themselves from plants and animals of the woodlands, river and prairies. This life was typical of the earliest pioneers, who combined European and Native American hunting and farming skills and lived in a way that was neither Old World nor New, but a successful mix.

Other families came into the neighborhood two years after the Coles. The settlers were able to clear more land, but it was not a peaceful existence. Illinois tribes had begun to raid Missouri settlements. The United States was busy in the East with the War of 1812, so Native Americans felt that there might be a chance to eliminate the pioneers.

In the summer, an Indian killed one of Hannah's neighbors who was out hunting. The settlers gathered at Stephen's cabin, only to find themselves surrounded. Samuel raised his rifle to fire, but Hannah put her hand on the barrel and lowered it, to stop him making the situation worse. There was a standoff.

While the settlers and Indians faced each other, a French trader in a boat came up the river. The French, allies of the Native Americans in the battle to get Americans out, routinely traded firearms and ammunition for furs. The settlers raided the French boat and took it across the river to Fort Kincaid, which had been recently built.

The settlers stayed in Fort Kincaid all winter and returned for spring planting. While they worked, they took turns standing guard and there were no more attacks in 1812 or 1813.

Still, their troubles were not over. In 1814, another settler was killed. The fort served as schoolhouse, church, post office, hospital and county seat. And as community leader, Hannah's success continued as more people came to settle. When there was need for a ferry across the river, Hannah got a license. Her sons ran the business. Hannah and her children left us no writings as they probably could neither read nor write. So we have no clear idea of what happened to the fort or her property as the town of Boonville grew. As she was a woman, her claim was tenuous, but there is some evidence that she was paid $100 for her land. At any rate, the children were grown and Hannah moved with Sam and his family to a farm that he purchased, farther away from town, but closer to the wilderness they loved.

When the railroad came through, Hannah's bluff was blasted away. Today, there is a stone marker near the spot. It says:

> "Hannah Cole
> A pioneer mother
> who established the first
> home south of the Missouri
> River and built a fort near
> this site in 1810."

"Colter flew, rather than ran . . ."

John Colter
First White Man in Yellowstone

On the two-year, four-month expedition to explore the newly acquired Louisiana Purchase with the Corps of Discovery, Private John Colter (1774-1813) was Lewis and Clark's Mr. Fix-It, the trusted assistant summoned to solve troublesome problems such as lost men and horses. As the expedition was making its return trip after reaching the Pacific Ocean, Colter went native. He received permission from Lewis and Clark to join two fur traders heading back up along the Missouri River and into the Northern Rockies — the land of Indians and beaver.

There he remained for almost six years. He trapped for skins, scalped his Blackfeet Indian foes (legend has it he chalked up 101) and tried to keep his own head away from tomahawks. The latter he did with such style that it became the stuff of legend, none more hair-raising than his flight, naked, from a band of 800 Blackfeet who, for their own sport, chased him like a pack of hunting dogs.

The following account of Colter's run (as it came to be known) was written by John Bradbury, an Englishman who met Colter near Dundee. In *Travels in the Interior of America,* he recounted how Colter and another lonely trapper named Potts

"were on a branch of the Missouri called Jefferson Fork and had set their traps at night, about six miles up a small river that emptied into the fork. Early in the morning they ascended the river in a canoe to examine the traps. The banks on each side were high and perpendicular and cast a shade over the stream. As they were softly paddling along, they heard the trampling of many feet upon the bank. Colter immediately gave the alarm of "Indians!" and was for instant retreat. Potts scoffed at him for being frightened by the trampling of a herd of buffaloes. Colter checked his uneasiness and paddled forward. They had not gone much farther when frightful whoops and yells burst forth from each side of the river, and several hundred Indians appeared on either bank. Signs were made to the unfortunate trappers to come on shore. They were obliged to comply. Before they could get out of their canoe a savage seized the rifle belonging to Potts. Colter sprang on shore, wrested the weapon from the hands of the Indian and restored it to his companion, who was still in the canoe, and immediately pushed into the stream. There was the sharp twang of a bow and Potts cried out that he was wounded. Colter urged him to come to shore and submit, as his only chance for life; but the other knew there was no prospect of mercy and determined to die game. Leveling his rifle, he shot one of the savages dead on the spot. The next moment he fell, himself, pierced with innumerable arrows.

"The vengeance of the savages now turned upon Colter. He was stripped naked and, having some knowledge of the Blackfeet language, overheard a consultation as to the mode of dispatching him, so as to derive the greatest amusement from his death. Some were for setting him up as a mark and having a trial of skill at his expense. The chief, however, was for nobler sport. He seized Colter by the shoulder and demanded if he could run fast. The unfortunate trapper was too well acquainted with Indian customs not to comprehend the drift of the question. He knew he was to run for his life, to furnish a kind of human hunt to his persecutors. Though in reality he was noted among his brother hunters for swiftness of foot, he assured the chief that he was a very bad runner. His stratagem gained him some vantage ground. He was led by the chief into the prairie, about 400 yards from the main body of savages and then turned loose to save himself if he could. A tremendous yell let him know that the whole pack of 800 Indians were off in full cry. Colter flew rather than ran; he was astonished at his own speed, but he had six miles of prairie to traverse before he could reach the Jefferson Fork of the Missouri. Prickly pear wounded his naked feet. Still he fled on, dreading each moment to hear the twang of a bow and to feel an arrow quivering at his heart. He did not even dare to look around, lest he should lose an inch of that distance on which his life depended. He had run nearly half way across the plain when the sound of pursuit grew somewhat fainter, and he ventured to turn his head. The main body of his pursuers was a considerable distance behind; several of the fastest runners were scattered in the advance; while a swift-footed warrior, armed with a spear, was not more than a hundred yards behind him.

"Inspired with new hope, Colter redoubled his exertions, but strained himself to such a degree that the blood gushed from his mouth and nostrils and streamed down his breast. He arrived within a mile of the river. A glance behind showed his pursuer within 20 yards and preparing to launch his spear."

And then it is related that Colter, despairing of escape, suddenly turned around and spread out his arms. The savage tossed his blanket away, seized his spear in both hands and lunged at Colter. But Colter grabbed the spear near the head, broke off the iron point, and the Blackfoot, thrown off his balance, crashed to the ground. Colter pinned his foe with the spearhead, jerked it out of the body, plucked up the blanket and was off.

There were yells and shouts as the vanguard of the pursuing army reached their fallen companion. Colter used that moment to good advantage. Coming to the edge of the stream that was his goal, he plunged through the willows on its banks and dived into the water. Not far away was a beaver house. Swimming underwater, he made for it, rose up into it and found a place inside the structure where he could breathe.

The Indians were soon crowding the banks of the stream. Peering through the vent in the side of the house, Colter could see his foes searching for hours before they went away.

Colter kept fast till midnight, then he dived into the stream again and swam silently for a considerable distance, when he landed. He kept on all night, and by daybreak he had traveled far enough to be out of immediate danger.

But he struggled along, traveling by day and night, stopping only for the most meager repose and attempting to nourish himself on roots and the bark of trees. Eleven days later he arrived at the fort. His feet had "swole" on the trip.

On another of Colter's footloose journeys, his trapping took him through present-day Yellowstone Park, where he may have been the first white man ever to witness the geysers of hot water gushing from the ground. The area was known as "Colter's Hell." In fact, his stories of geysers and sulphur-smelling water were so amazing that many considered him a liar.

To the astonishment of those who thought he'd been killed, Colter showed up in Missouri in 1810 and married. With William Clark, he drafted a map of the Northwest. The map was included in Biddle's 1814 edition of the Lewis and Clark journals. It shows a dotted line marked "Colter's Route."

Colter himself settled near Dundee, Missouri, with his wife. In 1926, 113 years after his death, a steam shovel digging along a Missouri River bluff uprooted what were thought to be his bones. A *St. Louis Post-Dispatch* reporter, alert to the find, discovered that the fierce frontiersman had been forgotten, even by his relatives. "Nobody knew much about him," Julius Kleimann reported after conducting a series of interviews with the Colter elders. "He had lived, started a family and died. A brief life and a short fame, apparently. Gone, it seemed, was his repute on the tongues of men. Nobody knew him."

In recent years, residents near Washington and New Haven, Missouri, have placed a monument to Colter atop the bluffs overlooking the Missouri River that first took him out west.

"My Daddy never refused to buy any horse I wanted, and I wanted many of them . . ."

Loula Long Combs
Early Horse Show Performer

"My Daddy never refused to buy any horse I wanted, and I wanted many of them." This line from an autobiography published in 1947 sums up one of the happiest, most privileged lives ever lived in Missouri. The book is *My Revelation,* the author Loula Long Combs of Lee's Summit, internationally known in her time as winning equestrienne, as well as the daughter of R. A. Long, one of the most successful businessmen in the history of our state.

Far from being the self-centered person she could have been, Loula Long Combs was sensitive to others, even to animals. She risked offending people by insisting that old show horses should be kept comfortably at home instead of being sold into lives of drudgery. She once went into a show ring to stop a class she considered unkind and degrading.

Mrs. Combs lived (1881-1971) during times of continuity and certainty. During her youth, her father's wealth was safe and she dwelt in a snug cocoon of love, her family deeply involved with private and public religion. Her writing is warmly appreciative of family, staff and friends. Her life is best described by a few vignettes from her book:

... a little girl in guilty agony for having said "damn" to a man beating his mule. Swearing was forbidden by Loula's Quaker mother, and the child didn't expect the boon of hearing that if anything ever justified cursing, it would be cruelty.

... a novice driver in wrinkled raincoat, in a muddy Canadian show ring, winning with a borrowed horse over an exquisitely turned out Vanderbilt.

... a fully bloomed young lady on her first trip to Europe (1910) driving in the Olympic Show in London. For this her own horse, with all its trappings and attendants, had crossed the ocean and they won, against 18 seasoned male drivers, leaving the ring to cries from the audience of "Hurrah for Missouri!"

... the kaleidoscoped decades of riding and driving beautiful show horses. With maturity, driving took precedence and Loula Long Combs began wearing flowing gowns of silk or velvet and wide-brimmed hats buoyant with feathers or flowers. A typically successful year was 1920, when she won $15,000 in prizes, 31 championships and 130 blue ribbons.

... finally, stout and 80 years old in 1961 and having acknowledged a standing ovation, leaving the American Royal show ring for the last time drawn by two beloved old campaigners brought in for the occasion from retirement pasture.

Such a level of horse activity is consuming, even for a person with plenty of money and plenty of helpers. Loula Long Combs had to practice and study, horse shop, travel and supervise staff. But to fully appreciate the balance she kept, one must know more about the estate that writers have called "Horse Heaven" and "a rural Versailles." Loula wrote, "Only by helping others could I express my thanks for having such a home."

On Longview Farm's 1,780 acres stood sixty buildings, most of them of matching cream stucco with red tile roofs. They included the three-floor 20-room family mansion, houses for many of Longview's 400 employees, greenhouses, barns for every kind of livestock and fowl, carriage houses and shops. There was even an animal hospital with resident veterinarian, and a picturesque chapel for use by all of Longview's residents. The estate had a 20-acre artificial lake, its own sewer system and underground conduits for electrical and telephone wires.

But what impressed horse-loving visitors most was the 36-stall barns for saddle and harness horses, with floors of hoof-friendly wooden brick and carpeted aisles for comfort and safety. An indoor driving arena measured 80 by 175 feet, and outdoors was a half-mile track with seating for a thousand spectators. Within Longview there were seven miles of road for pleasure riding and driving and for training. All this cost only a million dollars to build by 1914 values, and R. A. Long could afford it.

The farm's most serious focus was on show horses, which went all over the continent to compete; Longview horses were among the most famous in the country and their blood is still sought after. They justified hiring the country's best trainers. John T. Hook was brought from Mexico, Missouri, to oversee all that pertained to American Saddlebreds, and a harness horse ace was imported from England. When first occupied, Longview was the largest horse operation west of the Mississippi and for decades continued to set the standards, a formidable rival to the oldest, best-established southern stud farms. In 1942 when Pathe News wanted to do a documentary called "Show Horse" they came to Longview for twelve weeks of filming.

The life Loula lived was as idyllic as all this sounds. When she married, she chose a longtime family friend who understood her life with horses and supported it. One upsetting thing she did record was when she was taken literally: she had named a then-fantastic price for Chief of Longview, the best colt the Longs ever produced. This young stallion, strikingly beautiful and possessed of great show ring presence and perfection in gaits, had just made a debut so remarkable that people at the show wired friends and neighbors to come and see him. When asked jokingly what she would take for Chief, she replied in the same mode, "Oh, no less than $25,000!" This was an incredible price at the time, but to her dismay, it was not too much for Mrs. William Matson, wife of the shipping magnate, who insisted that the price had been named and the colt was hers. We are told that Loula and Chief's trainer and exhibitor, Lon Hayden, wept together when the animal was taken away. He did not do well for the Matsons, so they sent back to Longview for Lon. Thus Loula also lost one of her best employees, but she wanted Chief to have Hayden's care, and she took pride in all their prizes and championships.

Apart from horses, even after she became operator of the farm, Loula's interests and concerns included church, the children of her sister and her employees, a multitude of pets and charitable activities. Many charity shows were held at Longview, sometimes exhibiting just the farm's own horses.

In the seventieth decade of his life, R. A. Long's overextensions, coupled with changes in the economy, reduced his wealth to less than a million dollars. The farm was secure, however, and Loula and her sister, Sallie, lived out their lives as widows there. As they aged, they sold and gave away parts of Longview. One portion went as a site for a junior college to serve the area.

More recently, the corps of engineers flooded part of the estate, and the remainder, with its buildings, was converted for various uses. Though the saddle horse barn burned in 1977, many equine accommodations still are intact and are utilized for shows and meets by Missouri horse people.

Loula Long Combs, who took religion very seriously, ended her book with a vision of otherworldly bliss we can hope she found: "Green Pastures of surpassing loveliness, watered by crystal heavenly streams, where we may find again our animal friends. A dream you say? Who knows?"

"last of the village bards . . . his ear pitched to the accents of the common people . . ."

Jack Conroy
Poet of the People

At age eight, in Monkey Nest, a coal mining camp near Moberly where he was born in 1899, Jack Conroy first tested his literary legs. He began writing a four-page newspaper, the *Monkey Nest Monitor,* in lead pencil. The *Monitor* appeared irregularly, the sole copy scrawled on butcher paper.

Conroy absorbed what education he could from his readings of G. A. Henty and Horatio Alger novels and his sporadic attendance at Sugar Creek School. As a teenager in Moberly he worked by day at the Wabash Railway car shops and studied by night to pass high school correspondence courses. At age 21 Conroy enrolled in the University of Missouri, intending to major in literature, but left after a year, unable to stomach wartime military training.

After dropping out in 1921, Conroy hopped around the country in boxcars. To support himself, he worked at a steel mill in Des Moines, Iowa, and hauled paving stones on a road crew in Moberly.

While working a series of low-paying factory jobs, Conroy moonlighted as a writer and began to make his way onto the alternative literary scene. In 1927, while laboring at a rubber heel plant in Hannibal, Missouri, he struck up a friendship with the anarchist Ralph Cheyney, founder of the Rebel Poets and a World War I draft resister who had been jailed for his refusal to take up arms against the enemy. He and Cheyney collaborated on a number of projects; as joint editors, they issued three anthologies of protest poetry titled *Unrest.*

With the onset of the Depression, Conroy found his voice. Some of the new, avant-garde magazines of the day published his verse. He wrote stories on unemployment, which appeared in the *New Masses*, a socialist magazine. The crisp vigor of Conroy's style impressed H. L. Mencken, editor of the *American Mercury.*

Reduced to working one day a week at the Willys-Overland automobile plant in Toledo, Ohio, Conroy scrounged for odd jobs to feed his family. The struggle fueled his writing but did little to fill his pockets. The 1929 stock market crash drove the Conroys back to Moberly. There, they hoped, family would help them through lean times.

Conroy dated his start as an author from 1930, the year Mencken bought his story "Hard Winter" for $135. In Mencken, Conroy found a steady patron and adviser. He urged Conroy to cast his Depression sketches into book form and send them to his publisher, Alfred A. Knopf. Thirteen rejections followed. Finally, Covici-Friede, a New York publisher, agreed to publish Conroy's manuscript as a novel, if Conroy would agree to fictionalize the episodes and tie them together into a coherent story.

In the 1930s Conroy embarked on one of the most fruitful periods of his life. With Walter Snow, a New York editor and publicist, Conroy launched the *Anvil,* a magazine that published the works of unknown and prominent 20th-century American writers such as Nelson Algren and Richard Wright.

In 1933 Conroy's first novel, *The Disinherited,* was published to general acclaim. Partly autobiographical, it told the story of Larry Donovan, a down-and-out drifter who goes from job to job in Depression-era America. The novel was based in part on Conroy's own experiences, dressed up as fiction.

Though his reputation is largely based on his first novel, Conroy never considered himself a fiction writer. His goal in *The Disinherited,* he said, was to be "a witness to the times, to set down as truthfully as I could the things I had seen" (quoted by Anne Commire). His 1935 novel, *A World to Win,* was also based on his life experiences. "I'm not much of a creator," he told Robert Thompson, an interviewer for the *Missouri Review,* in 1983. "I just set down what I've seen or heard. Whatever I write, I have to have seen or come in close contact with, somehow or another. I don't see how some people can sit down and take a set of characters and some situations and weave them into a novel. I couldn't do that."

In 1935 Conroy was awarded a Guggenheim fellowship to study blue-collar migration from South to North. The next year his literary magazine, bedeviled by debt, was swallowed up by the *Partisan Review.* Conroy, hoping to revive the *Anvil* in one form or another, moved to Chicago in 1938. With Nelson Algren, he sponsored lectures and staged a beer-hall melodrama to raise money for the *New Anvil.* The magazine lasted almost two years before it folded with the May-June issue of 1940, the editors unable to rally financial support during the war.

Conroy took a job with the Federal Writers' Project in Illinois. In that capacity he collected stories from the factories and mines — so-called industrial folklore. With the assistance of the black novelist Arna Bontemps, a colleague at the Federal Writers' Project, he turned several of the tales into juvenile books.

The most famous of these, published in 1942 by Houghton Mifflin, was "The Boomer Fireman's Fast Sooner Hound," a story Conroy first heard in the Wabash Railway shops in Moberly. Cleaned up and reworked into *The Fast Sooner Hound*, the colorful story of a hound who outraces the powerful Wabash Cannonball Railroad, it became Conroy's most popular book, selling more than 200,000 copies. Conroy and Bontemps collaborated on two other juveniles: *Slappy Hooper, the Wonderful Sign Painter*, in 1946, and *Sam Patch—The High Wide and Handsome Jumper*, in 1951. In 1945, Bontemps and Conroy also wrote *They Seek a City*, a history of black migrations in America that was later revised and republished in 1966 as *Anyplace but Here,* which won the James L. Dow award from the Society of Midland Authors.

From 1947 until 1966, Conroy worked as an editor in Chicago for the *American People's Encyclopedia* and as senior editor for the *New Standard Encyclopedia.* After resigning, he returned to Moberly to write his autobiography. The first installment of his memoirs, "Home to Moberly," was published in 1968 in the *Missouri Library Association Quarterly.* Conroy followed this with five episodic tales about his days in Monkey Nest coal camp, the last written when he was 83 years old. His full autobiography was never completed.

Conroy was widely admired and liked, particularly by the young writers he encouraged. His official biographer, Douglas Wixson, described him as the "last of the village bards. He kept language alive and interesting in an age of declining literacy. He had his finger on the pulse of the community, his ear pitched to the accents of the common people. He collected sentimental verse and religious tracts, valuing them for their verbal peculiarities; he hated cant and would review an entire book in less than an hour. He was entirely devoted to writing but he disliked the actual task. First thinking the entire story out in his head, he would pull himself over to his battered, sweat-stained Underwood typewriter and, with his two index fingers flying, compose the first and final version, which he would check for misspellings."

In May 1985, Conroy was recognized by his hometown. About 500 admirers turned out for the Jack Conroy Day celebration, which featured Stephen Wade performing the Conroy folk tales he had adapted for the theater and used in his long-running show "Banjo Dancin'" in Washington, D.C. Conroy suffered a stroke in 1988 and spent the last two years of his life in a nursing home, unable to talk. He died on February 28, 1990, at the age of 91 and was buried in the miners' cemetery at Sugar Creek near Moberly.

She studied law . . . and was still a lady!

Phoebe Couzins
First Woman U.S. Marshal

At a time when the U.S. Supreme Court was giving bar associations permission to keep women from practicing law, Phoebe Couzins was blazing a trail that led, if not to the door of the courthouse, at least to the admissions office of law school.

Couzins was the first woman in the United States to graduate from law school. In 1871, she received her law degree from St. Louis Law School (now Washington University). Just two years earlier, in 1869, the U.S. Supreme Court concluded that women should be sheltered from the brutish masculine world of law practice.

Couzins was admitted to the bar of several states and practiced law briefly. Her elegance and decided femininity apparently helped dispel the idea that legal study would make a man of a woman.

In her middle years, Couzins channeled most of her energies into the fight for women's right to vote, becoming a member of the Woman Suffrage Association of Missouri. She represented the Missouri group as a delegate to the 1869 convention of the American Equal Rights Association, but later abandoned it after helping Susan B. Anthony and others form the more radical National Woman Suffrage Association. She also took up temperance work.

In 1887, Couzins succeeded her father as U.S. Marshal for the Eastern District of Missouri. She held the office for two months, filling in between her father's death and the selection of his replacement; presumably Couzins was thus the first woman ever to serve as a U.S. Marshal.

In her later years, Couzins turned her back on her causes. She renounced the suffrage movement and took a job as Washington, D.C., lobbyist and lecturer for the United Brewers' Association, a beer company trade group. In that position, she opposed laws regulating the sale and use of alcoholic beverages, a 180-degree shift from her days as a temperance crusader.

The man who drafted the law that drafted thousands

Enoch H. Crowder
Writer of the Military Code

Enoch H. Crowder — cigar-puffing, black-coffee-drinking, solitaire-playing army lawyer, whose sensitivity to language made a dictionary his frequent companion — drafted the controversial law in 1917 that reinstated military conscription in the United States.

General Crowder's proposed law was passed by Congress substantially unchanged in May 1917, a month after war was declared on Germany. The law gave the president of the United States authority to draft all males aged from 21 to 30 into military service.

Crowder also set up the administrative machinery for draft registration that resulted in the smooth and rapid selection of 687,000 men to make up the new national army.

During his army legal career Crowder's accomplishments included but were not limited to a stint as Judge Advocate of the American Expeditionary Force in the Philippines, where he served as military governor of the islands, a term as chief of the Department of State and Justice of Cuba's provisional government. He was also responsible for revising the U.S. Military Code.

"more than just an ordinary housewife . . ."

Pearl Curran
Puritan Channeler and Ghostwriter

Pearl Curran of St. Louis called herself "just an ordinary housewife." And on the surface, this seems an accurate description. She was happily married to a prosperous man; they had a nice home and a pleasant social life.

But Pearl Curran became internationally famous and still intrigues students of the paranormal for something that has never been explained. She apparently channeled the spirit of Patience Worth, a woman born in England in the 1600s, a Puritan immigrant killed by Indians.

Patience Worth announced herself through a Ouija board to Pearl Curran and her friend in the summer of 1913. The two regarded "Weedj" as just a novelty fad and were amazed when, after two weeks' occasional use brought almost nothing, the game's little marker suddenly begin moving briskly over its alphabet.

"Many moons ago I lived," it spelled out.
"Again I come. My name, Patience Worth."

Initially, the women were frightened, but Mrs. Curran's mother began jotting down a further string of letters. Studied and punctuated, these gave more information about the strange visitor.

The messages concerned Patience Worth's life in England and America and answered questions about death and the hereafter: Death was just "a blink, the sleep and the wakin'" and there is no reincarnation. Children often figured in poems and prayers Worth offered. Most memorable was her improvement on the traditional and frightening bedtime lines:

> "I, thy child forever, play
> About thy knees this close of day.
> Into thy arms I soon will creep
> And learn thy wisdom while I sleep."

Friends and neighbors whom the Currans had told of the phenomenon came regularly to witness it, and gradually the story spread until newspaper people were present. Then, from all over the United States came experts in archaic languages and the histories of Britain and colonial America. These people were baffled that the entity was absolutely accurate in all she said. Her language was correct for the time and place she claimed to come from. The best of her poems were of high quality, some sublime, some earthily humorous. Many were as pleasant as this:

> "The grey nun Night kneels:
> Atween her fingers the rosaries of stars
> Slip one by one."

Literary authorities agreed that Worth's work was good. Among those fascinated with the output was Caspar Yost, an editor at the *St. Louis Globe Democrat,* who believed Patience was a spirit; he later rejected the multiple personality theory. Had the latter been the answer, he pointed out, it still left the question of where the Worth writings came from. Yost published a five-part series on the mystery and later a book on Patience Worth that was bought by Henry Holt in New York and went through four printings. Holt then published two of Worth's novels.

Another respected St. Louisan who lent credence to Patience Worth was Marion Reedy, editor of *Reedy's Mirror,* a prestigious literary magazine with a circulation of 32,000, some of it in Europe. The first to publish many who became famous, he also published Patience Worth. Reedy dismissed the supernatural, but said the Currans lacked background, ability and motivation to perpetrate a hoax.

Pearl Curran soon received Patience without a companion at the Ouija board and then didn't even need the board. When Patience began sending novels and plays, Mrs. Curran simply sat and let letters and then words out as rapidly as she could speak. She said she received vivid images at the same time, like a colored movie.

In the first seven of her 25 years of association with Pearl Curran, Patience had spelled out about two million words; it was impossible to imagine anyone memorizing enough material daily to deliver this night after night. And the couple never profited from Patience. They spent thousands on shorthand stenographers and on efforts to publish Worth's work.

By our standard, most of the novels are too long and tiresome, language of Worth's day too stilted and flowery. Except for her poetry, Patience's published work never developed a popular following. Hoax charges continued and doubters investigated relentlessly. The Currans opened their home to searches for evidence that Pearl was somehow spending the days composing what she presented as Patience's work, that she or her husband was researching 17th-century Britain. Nothing was ever found. Public library books Mrs. Curran had used were only a few light novels.

Interviews with people everywhere Mrs. Curran had lived as she grew up confirmed the original picture, that she took no special interest in history, religion or writing. Never a good student, at 13 she'd had "a nervous breakdown." Her parents allowed her to drop out of school and her birthdate, 1883, explains that. Education for girls had low priority then.

All doubters conceded that even if she could compose the material or her husband could, the means of presentation were still inexplicable. It was customary for Patience to compose extemporaneous poems on themes guests suggested. Throughout, Mrs. Curran's friends and neighbors attested, she kept her usual schedule of visiting and shopping; when was she preparing her performances?

One factor to consider is that during adolescence, just after her "breakdown," Pearl Curran had lived in the Ozarks among people of British descent whose elders still used words and forms similar to Worth's. Had Pearl unconsciously taken this in? Had she absorbed British history, prayers and songs? But if so, again, how did she relay it in such quantity?

With urgings from Patience Worth, the Currans adopted a baby girl, and then in 1933, six months after her husband's death, Pearl gave birth to her own baby daughter. To earn their living, she did a little freelance writing, but it lacked the quality of Patience Worth's and markets soon dried up. She married twice more and died in California on Thanksgiving Day 1937, alone except for a female companion and her youngest daughter.

If Patience Worth had anything else to say, she hasn't found a suitable channel. Nothing more from her appears in annals of the apparently genuine paranormal. Whether Patience Worth was genuinely paranormal, or just a scam with John Curran's help or instigation, it is certain that Pearl Curran was much more than just an ordinary housewife.

"... described acorns as big as hen's eggs, and grapevines laden with sweet fruit ..."

Gottfried Duden
Founder of Missouri's Rhineland

In 1824, an optimistic traveler named Gottfried Duden, from Rhineland Germany, arrived on Missouri soil. He believed that many of Germany's crimes resulted from overpopulation and poverty. Thinking emigration was the key, Duden and his friend Louis Eversmann set sail for America to study the possibilities of German settlement in the United States. Duden kept a journal of his day-to-day experiences in Missouri and published a book that received great acclaim in Germany. Duden's words were to spark massive migrations of oppressed Germans to the Missouri River Valley. He was to stay, too, settling near present-day Dutzow.

As the Editor's Introduction of the University of Missouri Press English translation of Duden's book puts it:

> *The Report of a Journey to the Western States of North America* was a masterpiece of promotional literature. Duden's adroit pen wove reality with poetry, experience with dreams, and contrasted the freedom of the forests and democratic institutions in America with the social narrowness and political confusion of Germany. He glorified the routine of pioneer existence, praised Missouri's favorable geographical location, and emphasized its mild and healthy climate. He dwelt on the benevolence of its nature and the abundance of its fish and wildlife, and contrasted Germany's poverty and hunger with America's plenty. So overwhelmed with what he saw and experienced, Duden feared Germans would not believe him: "It appears," he wrote, "too strange, too fabulous."

Upon arriving in St. Louis, they were directed to Nathan Boone, son of Daniel Boone and surveyor of government lands (also featured in this book). Duden and his companion were then given a tour of the Missouri River Valley by Boone. Upon leaving several days later, the two men lost their way and headed west instead of east. Soon they arrived at the house of Jacob Haun, of Pennsylvania German descent. Haun talked them into purchasing adjoining land and offered to shelter and feed them until they could establish their own farms. Duden agreed to purchase the land so he could better judge the German experience in Missouri.

For the next two years, Duden lived in a cabin near Lake Creek and recorded the daily doings on his farm. Since he did not engage in any profession or trade, however, his simple experience did not echo many of the hardships that would await true pioneering German families.

In 1829, Duden took his diary and published a best-seller back in Germany, entitled *Report of a Journey to the Western States of North America and a stay of several years along the Missouri (during the years 1824, 25, 26, 1827)*, in which he described the fertile Missouri River Valley and its likeness to southern Germany.

Though his book gave a detailed day-to-day log of building a home from the wilderness, he failed to mention the hardships awaiting incoming settlers. A cholera epidemic spread up and down the river valley during the 1840s and 1850s; flooding reached devastating levels in 1844 and civil war bushwackers raided many pioneer communities along the river during the 1860s.

But his writings did stir the restless and romantic souls of Germany.

"I do not conceal the fact from you that the entire life of the inhabitants of these regions seemed to me like a dream at first," wrote Gottfried Duden. "Even now, after I have had three months to examine conditions more closely, it seems to me almost a fantasy when I consider what nature offers man here." Duden described acorns as big as hen's eggs, and grapevines laden with sweet fruit.

To the struggling, even starving, German-speaking European at home, the allure of freedom and plenty in America was irresistible. This glowing (and exaggerated) account inspired thousands of Germans to emigrate to the "New Rhineland."

Settlement communities were organized. Both Hermann and Washington, Missouri, were founded by these settlement societies, and they are still well known for their German culture and architecture. Here settlers could perpetuate their customs, handicrafts and hillside agriculture undisturbed by the tensions and strife that plagued the German states in the 19th century.

Settling mostly along the Mississippi River south of St. Louis and the Missouri River from St. Louis to Boonville, especially south of the river, they created what one geographer calls the "German Arc." That area along the Missouri River is often referred to, even today, as "The Missouri Rhineland."

German-speaking settlers often named their settlements for the places they had left. In Perry County, Missouri's first German Lutheran immigrants (1839) arrived, partly inspired by Duden's book. They created Altenburg, Dresden, Frohna, Seelitz and Wittenberg, named for towns in Germany. Other German place names are sprinkled around the state: Detmold, Dissen, Hermann, Kiel and New Offenburg, for example.

Duden wrote, “if a little city could be founded, for the purposes of making it the center of culture in America, then there would be a rejuvenated Germania and the European Germans would then find in America a Second Fatherland.” To many German Americans living in Missouri, Hermann is considered the town of Duden’s dream and the Missouri Rhineland the Second Fatherland.

Besides bringing their place names, the settlers brought religion, music, foods, industry and tradition with them. Many years before the Christmas tree was adopted by Anglo settlers, there are records of that tradition in German Missouri homes.

Some German-speaking settlers pledged that they would retain their language and customs, but most families came to the territory determined to become productive Americans. They often named their towns with idealistic or patriotic names such as Freedom, Hope, Liberty, Useful and Welcome.

By the Civil War, dozens of rural German communities were in place, complete with schools, churches, fraternal organizations, stores and post offices. Generally abolitionists, the German-speaking Missourians found themselves at odds with the southern settlers who had come before. Missouri was particularly divided during the Civil War.

During World War I, with anti-German feeling strong, many German Americans felt they should assert their American identities. The German language was abandoned in schools and churches and some residents of German places felt they should change their names. Madison County’s German Township became Marquand; Gasconade County’s town of Potsdam became Pershing. There were motions to change the name of Bismarck to Loyal and Kaiser to Success. Citizens of Diehlstadt considered changing its name to Liberty. These three changes were resisted.

By World War II, the descendants of these German Americans felt rightly secure in their homeland. The German names on our landscape have endured as markers in our history.

A middle man of “munificent” means

Charles D. Eitzen
Early Civic Booster

In 1837-1838, when the settlers came streaming in from Pennsylvania to what was to become the little town of Hermann, Missouri, one of the early arrivals was a young man, not yet in his teens, named Charles Eitzen. He immediately took to work at the Wiedersprecher store on Wharf Street. What no one could foresee was that this young man would become the outstanding entrepreneur of the entire settlement. Whether he knew of John Jacob Astor and his strong-arm control of the fur trade of the Upper Missouri River or not, Eitzen certainly was going to develop comparable skill in the money-making business.

Within two years, the store owner became ill and Eitzen became the owner. The Missouri River flowed almost by the door of the store and Eitzen watching it flow saw endless possibilities. Where others viewed the river as a formidable barrier, Eitzen saw only opportunity.

Rafts of pine lumber were already flowing from the mouth of the Gasconade River, just seven miles upriver. Eitzen became the agent, selling lumber locally for the rapidly expanding town. He also began transshipping lumber to St. Louis and points further east. At times, he had thousands of feet of pine lumber stored along Wharf Street.

Eitzen also watched the struggle of the Maramec Iron Works in St. James to ship iron blooms from the foundry. Various rivers were tried: the Gasconade would only permit steamboats within 25 miles of the Paydown road leading to the foundry, the Meramec was too shallow. (Yes, there are two spellings, and both are correct. It is the Meramec River and the Maramec Iron Works.) Keelboats were too small and too slow, and even these cumbersome craft could often not make it through. Finally, the Iron Road was built from the ironworks to Hermann. Eitzen was ready. He became the agent for iron. Again, he was the transshipment agent, sending the 100-pound blooms on to Cincinnati, Wheeling and Pittsburgh. About two tons was the usual load for a team of 4-8 yoke of oxen.

The term "double dipping" might easily apply to Eitzen in the iron ore business. The great wagons bringing in the ore from Hermann did not go back empty. Eitzen saw that each returning wagon was heavily laden with all the amenities needed by the residents of "Stringtown" down at the ironworks — from his store, of course.

Eitzen remained in the iron ore business from 1840 to 1860, when a new railroad was constructed close to the ironworks. Eitzen, too, had used the Pacific Railroad for some of his transshipment business after the railroad was built through Hermann in 1855.

His final great undertaking was literally presented to him. In the early 1850s, the Pacific Railroad was starting to build track across Missouri and on to the western states. Eitzen was ready. Ties came out of the Gasconade River and he became the local agent to handle the rafts locally and sell the ties to the railroad company. In 1996, the track still ran between the river and Wharf Street in downtown Hermann, with nearly 40 fast trains roaring through daily. It is now called the Union Pacific Railroad, and four Amtrak passenger trains stop daily, a true asset to Hermann's thriving tourism industry.

Controversy was as palpable to Eitzen as success. However, it was not until he reached middle age that he began to face opposition. In his early years, the entire waterfront area had been his to rule with an iron fist. Steamboats regularly landed there and were welcome because they carried his goods to market. But when local interests began to encourage local steamboats, the fireworks began. Eitzen fought tirelessly to keep control of the waterfront, but he failed. Other boat companies flourished, the ferry business was very successful and the boat owners demanded, and got, wharf space and warehouse space.

One of the leading steamboatmen of that period was Capt. Heckmann. Eitzen and Heckmann were neighbors on Wharf Street for the greater part of their lives, but they were always enemies. They used Letters to the Editor to voice their differences and the editorials took sides. This was a very vocal ongoing argument.

The local newspaper — first the German-language *Volksblatt* and later the English-language *Advertiser Courier* — often criticized Eitzen and did not always uphold him when he ran for public office. The local people suspected that Eitzen was prospering, but no one had any idea of the extent of his holdings. When he died a millionaire in 1896, suddenly everything changed. With his death, the reading of his will shocked the town into a sudden and vociferous declaration of his "virtues." The *Advertiser Courier* did the proper thing:

> "It is needless to say that his munificent gifts to the county, to the school, the churches, the town — was and is the sole topic of conversation everywhere in the county since the provisions of his last will became known. Everybody feels honored in living in a community which was the home of a man like Chas. D. Eitzen. Many who spoke disparag-

ingly of his frugal habits and his great wealth now freely acknowledge that he was the 'noblest Roman of them all,' and that they did not know what they were talking about."

The "munificent" gift to Gasconade County was $50,000 to build a new courthouse on the site of the existing one. The unexpected also happened. Gasconade County is a long, skinny county and the location of the courthouse at the northernmost edge had long been a matter of argument with the middle and south county residents. Obviously, in horse and buggy days, a trip of some 50 miles to the courthouse to conduct legal business was difficult and many thought the center of county government should be located in the center of the county.

Eitzen's bequest had several stipulations. The courthouse had to be built within a specified time period and at the specified location or the money would revert to the estate. This precipitated a countywide vote — "Should the courthouse be moved?" The results were two-to-one in favor of the proposed Hermann location and the building was constructed in record time.

Today, the Gasconade County Courthouse stands as a remarkable monument to an energetic and civic-minded man. As far as is known, this courthouse is the only one in the state of Missouri, and the only one in the nation, to be built with private funds.

"I fancied . . . it was a sort of German Venice, having . . . canals filled . . . with foaming beer . . ."

Henry Theophilus Finck
Renaissance Man

Finck was a musician, a prominent editor and militant music critic for the *Nation* and *New York Evening Post*, an epicure, an aesthete, a professional pleasure seeker, professor, writer extraordinaire and author of many books on music, psychology, gardening and gastronomy, including *Gardening with Brains, Food and Flavor, Girth Control, Romantic Love and Personal Beauty, Songs and Song Writers, Chopin and Other Musical Essays.*

Finck prefaced his joyous autobiography, *My Adventures in the Golden Age of Music*, with the following note to readers:

> "Goethe called his autobiography 'Truth and Fiction.' Mine differs from his in that it is all truth and nothing but the truth. Not the whole truth, I confess. No mention is made in it of my frequent narrow escapes from the gallows or the electric chair or lynching. No reference is made to my hold-ups of California stages, my bold burglaries and midnight murders, my outrageous conduct at petting parties, my frequent elopements with other men's wives, and so on. Concerning such incidents there is so much in the daily papers that I feared my readers would yawn if I told them all my criminal adventures. Should there be an unexpected call for these scandalous details it will be easy to supply them in a second volume, same size as this, to be called 'The Whole Truth' or 'The Real Henry T. Finck.'"

He was born in Bethel, Missouri, on September 22, 1854. His father, Henry Conrad Finck, a druggist and amateur musician, trained the village band and choir.

At the outbreak of the Civil War, Union and Confederate troops passed through Bethel. Fighting erupted in Palmyra, not far away. Soon afterward his father, a widower with five children, moved his family to Oregon. At the time of the move, Finck was eight.

In 1862, the Finck family settled in the village of Aurora Mills, Oregon, 29 miles south of Portland, near a utopian colony organized by Wilhelm Keil and populated with Missouri transplants. Keil, a religious leader, had started the colony in 1844 in Bethel, Missouri, and had moved west with his followers in 1855.

Finck's father bought a house and an apple orchard. The family harvested up to 2,000 bushels of apples a year, selling them by the box through commission merchants. Finck loved Oregon apples, praised them to the heavens and believed his testimony as to their tastiness should be given exceptional weight because he had always been an ultra epicure, almost like a dog in the keenness of his sense of smell, on which the enjoyment of fruit and all food chiefly depends.

Though as a boy he deplored Oregon's lack of civilization, Finck in retrospect celebrated its roughness. His memoirs glow with nostalgia for the state, still a wild and woolly place when he got there in pre-railroad days. He gloried in the salmon, the mountains, the music, the fruit, and the Chinook wind. "How I used to enjoy that exhilarating wind! We had a pet lamb which, when that wind blew, used to put its four hoofs together and hop around like a crazy kangaroo till the whole Finck family was doubled up with laughter."

Finck's juvenile occupations in Aurora Mills included hunting pretty girls, stealing slices of smoked venison ham from Dr. Keil's smokehouse, reading Latin, writing in his diary (in Latin), banging a snare drum in a marching band, and playing his violincello with musicians in and outside the family.

Finck's memoirs portray a boy with a perenially empty stomach, overactive salivary glands, and an exceptionally full mind. He was passionate about music, though his refined sensibilities generally made him shudder at the toe-tapping tastes of his boorish contemporaries. At 16, he was a devotee of the highbrow styles. Schubert's songs moved him to shed tears of ecstasy, while his scorn was aroused by the cacophony that passed for popular music. Ever the critic, he hyperventilated over Mozart and Haydn and Beethoven and excoriated the lower forms. In the diary he kept as a young man one catches a glimpse of him sharpening his claws: "Brass band music," he wrote, "has this peculiarity that it always reminds me of a threshing machine through which live cats are being chased."

Finck prepared for college with the help of Christopher W. Wolf, graduate of the University of Göttingen. When Wolf heard that he was getting up before five o'clock in the morning, "in order to prepare myself for college by learning Latin and Greek, all by my lonely self," he took pity on him and kindly offered to teach him, "— free, of course," Finck wrote. "It was the most fortunate thing that ever happened to me in all my long life. For Wolf not only taught me the old languages, but he helped to open my eyes to the countless beauties of nature about us."

Together Finck and Wolf studied French, Latin, Greek, botany and astronomy, with Wolf sometimes coming by his house at two or three in the morning to show him a constellation visible only at that hour.

Finck's education in Oregon helped him pass the entrance examinations at Harvard University, which he began to attend in the early 1870s.

As a teenager in Oregon, Finck had admired Harvard from afar, writing in his diaries: "Can scarcely wait for the time when I shall go to Harvard University and have so many chances of seeing and learning things. I don't see why we should sit here at the 'end of the world,' where there is scarcely a civilized and refined human being to be found, when we might as well be elsewhere and have the benefit of good music and education, and innumerable things."

But the cross-country move caused him homesickness. When he got to Cambridge, Massachusetts, he missed Mount Hood, the Cascade Range, the Columbia River, and Oregon's big trees. As an older man, Finck concluded that his education in Oregon was superior to the "bench drilling" he got at Harvard, Heidelberg and Berlin. Though Finck studied music at Harvard during the 1870s under J. K. Paine, he specialized in philosophy and psychology. He credited one of his Latin teachers with helping him develop his pure, forceful writing style. He also studied the art of writing on his own. He bought two copies of Bartlett's *Quotations* and ripped the pages out of one of the copies. He carried the pages around in his pockets and in his spare moments he read them.

This is how he became thoroughly familiar with the world's best thoughts expressed in the most elegant and forcible style. At some of those thoughts, expressed so subtly, he felt like shouting for joy. They affected him like exquisite music. Finck's skill at playing violincello opened doors for him; doors, in some cases, that were well worth opening. The famous poet Henry Wadsworth Longfellow invited him to Christmas dinner, and he visited with America's foremost novelist at the time, William Dean Howells, editor of the *Atlantic Monthly,* who then hired Finck while still a student to review books on musical and philosophical subjects.

Finck graduated from Harvard in 1876 with the highest honors in philosophy. With a $500 loan from his Uncle Conrad, Finck traveled to Germany to cover the Wagner Festival in Bayreuth for the *New York World* and the *Atlantic Monthly*. There, he ran into the great man of opera himself, in front of the opera house one morning, and wangled an invitation to watch the festival rehearsals.

Finck, who was later to write an appreciative two-volume work on Wagner's life and operas, drank in the scene, watching "the great master superintending every detail of the performance." It was, Finck wrote, "a wonderful experience for me this, to be in the very workshop of the greatest operatic genius the world has ever known."

Finck decided to remain in Germany with $75 he had earned from his writing. There he traveled, loafed and savored the liquid cuisine and the music.

Writing of his move to Munich, he recalled: "Like most tourists I fancied, when I went to Munich that it was a sort of German Venice having, in place of streets, canals filled, not with sea water but with foaming beer on which the natives steered about on gondolas drawn by swans with long sausage necks, while the futurist musicians of the Wagner-mad Ludwig II played 'Lohengrin' from the roofs of the tallest houses on both sides of the canals."

Finck became a beer connoisseur, frequenting the Hofbrauhaus and the Pschorr, washing down dinners of black bread and sausage with mugs of the best ale in the world. He immersed himself in Munich's musical atmosphere, which included beer-hall concerts, and open-air performances by the king's military band. By flashing his newspaper clippings, Finck was able to attend the opera as an American correspondent. After a year, Finck, then 22, won a Harris Fellowship, which enabled him to study psychology and anthropology for three years in Berlin.

Finck's career as a journalist began in earnest in 1881 when E. L. Godkin, editor of the *Nation* and the *New York Evening Post,* hired him as music editor for both the magazine and the newspaper. Though he had hoped to become a philosophy professor, Finck recognized that philosophy professors are not supposed to be 25 years old, and he decided to write full-time instead.

As a journalist, Finck excelled. His duties included clipping and translating articles from the French and German press and covering the musical life of New York City. Though some of the city's morning dailies tried to lure him away from the *Post* with offers of more money, he remained at the New York evening daily, in part because he preferred to get a good night's sleep and write during the day. At the *Post*, Finck especially enjoyed talking music with Carl Schurz, a fellow Missourian and one of the newspaper's editors.

Finck, an occasional contributor to other journals, brought verve, wit and originality to his work. In 1887 he published *Romantic Love and Personal Beauty*, a book explaining his theory that romantic love was unknown in ancient nations. Writing about short songs, he pointed out and criticized the unfortunate tendency to esteem a work of art according to its bulk — what he called Jumboism. Finck explained his approach to music criticism in the preface to his book *Songs and Song Writers* (1900). "The most important function of musical criticism is, in my opinion, discovering and calling attention to good things the merits of which are not sufficiently known to the public, and to arouse enthusiasm for them."

During his tenure at the *Post* (1881-1924) Finck championed the work of Schubert, Wagner, Liszt, Grieg and MacDowell and criticized Brahms and Strauss, among others. In 1890 he was appointed Professor of Musical History at the National Conservatory in New York. He died in 1926, leaving a legacy of superb writing. In his autobiography, Finck recalled a chance encounter with novelist Mark Twain at the home of Richard Watson Gilder, editor of the *Century* magazine. Finck approached Twain and said: "Mr. Clemens, probably you don't know that you and I are the two great Missouri authors. To be sure, *I* don't amount to much but you make up the average."

He added, "If I had any sense, I would have said, 'To be sure *you* don't amount to much but I make up the average.' That would have made him think I, too, had a sense of humor."

the more animals around him the better

William Preston Hall
The World Was His Circus: Horse (and Elephant) King

He wore $20,000 worth of diamonds on his shirt, and crowds gathered to watch him work, large and imposing in silk top hat, leaning on a gold-headed cane, gesturing grandly to multitudes of horses: "No, not that one" or "Yes, this one."

He was William Preston Hall of Lancaster, Missouri, and his titles included "Diamond Billy" and "the lightning horse buyer." Hall called himself "Horse King of the World," though he could also have called himself "Elephant King."

A Schuyler County farmboy, born in 1864 and orphaned at 14, Hall hired himself out as farmhand, for board and one dollar a week. He somehow saved enough money in a year to buy a horse and hired it and himself out to a livery stable in Lancaster to earn and learn what he could. Within five years, Hall was the biggest buyer and seller of horses in the country.

In 1882, he'd met a large-scale dealer from Pennsylvania who recognized Hall's talent for evaluating horses and urged him to capitalize on it. He promised to buy the first boxcarful Hall would choose for his purposes and ship east. Hall became supplier for several dealers and soon was furnishing all the horses that American Express Company used west of Missouri. No one has offered any explanation as to how this young man could learn what usually takes decades of handling many types of horses to learn.

Probably few realize how incredible it was that he could judge soundness and capability at all, much less so rapidly. Most judges walk all around a horse and watch it move before venturing an opinion. It would be interesting to know how Hall explained his ability.

He was probably too busy to even think about it, for he pioneered transcontinental shipment of horses, supplying stock for the British Cavalry. During the Boer Wars (1880-1902), Hall established a depot in Cape Town, North Africa, for receiving horses he sent in lots of 2,000, channeling them on for military use. Hall put his brother, Louis, in charge of this operation.

This depot contributed to the second half of Hall's career, his traffic in elephants. In 1904 he bought his first circus, and after that — except for his getting very rich by finding horses for the Allies in World War I — his doings are hard to follow. Fred Pfening III recounts them in an article in the *Missouri Historical Review*.

Hall apparently began by bailing out stranded shows, buying some that were bankrupt, juggling equipment and animals around to create new shows and providing winter quarters at his multi-barned, many-acred establishment for animals and vehicles. At least once he lent his name to a circus and spent some time traveling with it. Often he owned more than one big show.

Hall might have been a master of opportunism, but he stayed with the circus business most of his life and it seems to have been a factor in his financial decline. After his death, Hall's son remarked, "My father would probably have been better off if he had not become interested in shows."

Though Hall is quoted to have said "The more animals I have around me, the better I like it," elephants captivated him most. He bought them from failed shows, took them as collateral on loans, traded for them, had many imported from Africa, sold them, leased them out. At peak, he had 32 elephants on his property at one time.

By some accounts he was solicitious of their well-being, for he went to Denver, Colorado, in July of 1913 to repossess four of his elephants when the Buffalo Bill–Pawnee Bill Show went bankrupt. The animals had been traveling since 1906 and each was worth at least $1,500.

One of the most interesting Hall stories was told by Monroe Cauble, who had bought a baby or dwarf elephant from Hall. Baby Bill proved a problem, however, accepting attention only from Cauble and one other person, and if both got out of its sight, it "would carry on something awful" (to quote Cauble). Cauble wired Hall and was told to return the animal and choose a replacement. Taking Baby Bill back was a problem because he needed a heated boxcar and could not be alone; both requirements were beyond the railroad. After some tense delays and threats to the railroad's national offices, claiming Little Bill was worth $4,000, Cauble got suitable accommodations for the creature he spoke of as "my baby." When they arrived at Lancaster at 11 o'clock at night in bitter cold, Hall was waiting at the depot.

Pfening's article quotes people who said that Hall was kind and responsible about all his animals, permitting no harshness or neglect from any of his employees. It's hard to take this too seriously, in view of his years of shipping horses off to be killed in war (history says that the Boer Wars killed 326,073 animals, 67 percent of those just from poor care and poor management), and sentencing all sorts of animals to the stresses and discomforts of circus life. On one occasion, he collected $8,000 from a show in which three elephants burned to death.

But regardless, Hall helped, for decades, to provide memorable entertainment for thousands of people. The World's Fair in St. Louis in 1904 featured "The Boer Wars Extravaganza," a reenactment using real veterans from both sides of the conflict, and hundreds of horses Hall supplied. Performances were done in an amphitheater big enough for realistic cavalry charges. Among the horses used were some that would convincingly play dead, some who crawled around as if injured, and one who dived from a high point of land into water. Hall wintered these animals at his place after the fair closed and was involved in a plan to take the reenactment on the road that spring. Unfortunately the tour soon folded because the soldiers, old hostilities renewed, began fighting for real.

Among audiences who enjoyed Hall's operations were fellow residents of Lancaster. Pfening quotes one neighbor who said it was like living on The Pike (midway) of the World's Fair. A typical Hall spectacular occurred one Sunday when, right after church, he took a team of six beautiful spotted horses into an open field with a giant calliope. It was their first experience with the bulk and the shrieking whistles (calliopes were like enormous steam-driven pipe-organs) of what they would pull. From parts of two calliopes, he had created what would be, for a while, the country's largest.

When he died in 1932, William P. Hall was reportedly $50,000 in debt, but he was possessed of a great deal of land, with quantities of animals and circus equipment. Now his many barns are gone and a home sits on the site. When Pfening wrote his article, the only reminders of Hall's operations were the elephant rings set in concrete behind the house. It is hard to imagine quiet where so much excitement and color once reigned, by order of one of the most flamboyant and busy men who ever lived in Missouri.

"By this time the Missouri River was getting rather full of Heckmanns . . . "

William Lewis Heckmann
Steering Missouri's Largest Riverboat Family

He was tall, handsome, charismatic — a man who collected people. He was a loving and faithful husband, a dyed-in-the-wool male chauvinist who sired 15 children (six girls and nine boys). His great voice graced the ranks of the Hermanner Harmonie, the male singing society. His presence was sought by all local organizations. His influence was enormous in the opening up of the state of Missouri via the Missouri River.

This man was born in 1845 on Wharf Street in Hermann, Missouri. The christening records show that he was originally named Johann Judwig Wilhelm Heckmann. By the time he reached school age, however, he was recorded by the americanized version. Lewis of the Lewis and Clark Expedition apparently influenced his young thinking and the name became William Lewis Heckmann.

Young Bill had the Missouri River for a front yard, no doubt a factor in his fascination with the river. Originally he followed his father's vocation and became a carpenter, a successful builder of houses and bridges and finally the buildings of the Bluffton Weinery. The Heckmann family at Hermann had a neighbor who became quite wealthy, a fact not unobserved by young Bill Heckmann who resolved to do the same. He was successful as a carpenter, but this was not remunerative enough. He became a steamboatman and promptly invested all the money he had made as a carpenter in a steamboat, actually two steamboats — and went broke.

His next venture was to join forces with the Wohlt family in the ferry and small freight business. Here he could put his carpentry skills into boat building as well as piloting and he became an expert at both. Some of the little boats owned by this company paid for themselves several times over in one season. They were the little steamers that opened up the interior of the state of Missouri before trucks and good roads were even dreamed of. One of these little steamers went up the Gasconade River to Arlington — now Jerome, near Rolla, Missouri, a once-in-forever trip. The ferry company was officially incorporated in 1880 as the Hermann Ferry and Packet Company and continued operation until 1935 when the last boat was sold.

Here again Bill Heckmann could not be satisfied. His namesake son wrote, "In his early life he was always organizing something. No silver or gold dollars [would] ever go dull in his pockets. He kept his dollars working and he hired hundreds of people."

Up on the Gasconade River all boatmen could not help but see the Pryor Mill. This was the *Lorelei*, beckoning to all who passed. Bill Heckmann was no exception, but he did something about it. He bought the mill and farm, sold all his boat stock and went into business on dry land. He put the most state-of-the-art machinery into the mill, built a miller's house and restored the spacious house on the farm for his still growing family. He spent $35,000 on the project, mostly borrowed.

The captain may have been a genius at steamboating, but he was not an astute businessman. He had visions of hauling all the wheat on the Gasconade River to the mill on his steamboats and bringing back the flour. He built two steamboats to accomplish this goal. It was a beautiful dream but the captain did not study his market. The flour was excellent but no buyers could be found. Also, when his own wheat from his farms was all ground, no other wheat appeared for grinding. What had happened — steam roller mills were springing up all around the area making it easier for the farmer to get his grinding done. Whereas the mill had once been the only means of securing flour within a 15-mile radius, now there were 15 within the same territory. The writing was on the wall.

The family moved back to Hermann. The captain traded one of his boats for stock in the ferry company and sold the other for cash and listed the mill and farm for sale. There were no buyers.

As the oldest Heckmann sons grew up and became pilots, their father always had a boat to "learn" on and then a boat to pilot. He had taken these three sons out of school at age 13 to learn the river. At the time of the move back to town the three oldest boys were running their own boats and doing well.

The captain had bought some 2,000 acres of prime farmland on the Missouri River islands. The spring of 1903 gave promise of bumper crops when along came the greatest flood ever known on that part of the river and wiped out all of the farmland, crops, buildings, machinery, everything. Financially, it wipe out the captain also.

The birth of the first three boys was followed by four girls and then four boys. Eventually, the younger boys, four of them, came to the age of learning on the river. Bob was 21 at the time of the flood, already through high school. He was teaching and was definitely not interested in steamboats. Ed, at 19, was just getting his license as a pilot and there were no boats waiting for him. George, at 17, was eagerly learning all he could about machinery in order to become a first-class engineer and John, at 15, was "cubbing" to learn to be a pilot.

By the time their father died in 1907 all four boys were working. Ed worked on the Missouri and on the White River in Arkansas and then took off for Alaska to pilot on the Yukon for four seasons. John, another pilot, became a steamboat owner at a very young age. George soon made his reputation as a top-notch engineer, an inventive genius.

Another son, Joseph, died in infancy and Norman, the baby, was only 12 when his father died so he did his "learning" to become a marine engineer from his brothers and the Wohlt family. Whether engineering was his first choice is debatable since he was too color blind to pass for his pilot's license.

By this time the Missouri River was getting rather full of Heckmanns. For many years it was not an uncommon sight to see four or five steamboats on the river, within sight of each other, each with at least one Heckmann on board, sometimes two, since the engineers often worked on the boats along with the pilots. One of the sons, Fred, held both a pilot's and an engineer's license and was equally good at both jobs.

Only one son, the genius marine engineer, ever developed a real affection for the diesel boats — the others remained steamboatmen to the core, although as times changed they had to adapt to the diesels. Three of the brothers never owned a car or learned to drive. They wanted nothing to do with an internal combustion engine. One claimed he would not fly until they put a steam engine in an airplane.

All of the Heckmann progeny worked on the river improvement projects at some time. Boats were essential to these projects, and the Heckmanns played a big role in the development of the Missouri River for navigation.

Capt. William Lewis Heckmann certainly had no idea he was creating a veritable steamboat dynasty and making a contribution to the history of his state, but he had a good time doing it. He died in 1907, broke again.

"She knocked out the wall of the attic, installed windows, had her studio, and was in the art business"

Anna Kemper Hesse
Guardian of Missouri's Past

Inadvertently, the little town of Hermann was put on the tourism circuit by a shy country girl. Some of the architectural preservation that makes Hermann so attractive to tourists can also be traced to her efforts. Anna Kemper Hesse has been a one-woman dynamo of ideas, talents and energy. A noted artist, writer, historian, taxidermist, horticulturist, lecturer and preservationist, her accomplishments are awe-inspiring.

Anna Hesse was born on the Kemperhof Farm, near Hermann, Missouri, on March 13, 1908. Youngest of three daughters, she became the right-hand "man" for her father on the farm as her older sisters married and left. She had graduated from eighth grade from the rural, one-room Coles Creek School. This precluded going to high school so she completed that by correspondence. After her high school correspondence work, she received an art scholarship for another correspondence course, and this led to the need for a studio. Undaunted, she undertook a carpentry project that might have stumped a man. She knocked out the wall of the attic, installed windows, had her studio, and was in the art business. This led to another correspondence course in taxidermy. This brought in enough money to pay for a year at the University of Missouri, Columbia.

Art classes under Anna were always full and out of this teaching came the organization of the Brush and Palette Club of Hermann. "The club was dedicated: (1) to create an interest in art, crafts, culture and history, and (2) to preserve and maintain some of the old and distinctive houses in the Hermann Area and in Gasconade County, Missouri, to the end that the whole shall be a memorial to the character of the Hermann Area Colonists and their culture." To this day the Brush and Palette Club sponsors the annual Arts and Crafts Fair in October.

Anna saw the need to restore the Rotunda in the City Park — they wanted to use it for art exhibits. Money for this restoration was lacking but a revival of the old Maifest (May Festival) remedied that. To the amazement of the Brush and Palette Club, the Maifest was an overwhelming success. Tourists poured in from all over the state, the town ran out of food and the artists realized they were into something far greater than they had anticipated. Tourism was born with a bang, and so was the organization Historic Hermann, Inc. The latter was to handle the Maifest and cope with the hordes of people who found Hermann such an attraction.

Today the Maifest is an annual event on the third weekend in May, bringing in around 25,000 tourists a day. Other "fests" have grown out of this idea and the Oktoberfest brings in a like number of tourists every weekend during that month. Daily Amtrak stops bring visitors the year around, charter buses are a common sight. Tourism has grown into a multimillion-dollar business in this little German town of less than 3,000!

Anna married Clarence Hesse, another fine artist. These two worked with the Brush and Palette Club to buy and restore the Pommer-Gentner and the Strehly houses in Hermann and opened them to tours. These historic homes have now been given to and are managed by the State of Missouri through the Department of Natural Resources, which, with the addition of another house as headquarters, established "Deutschheim" (Home of the Germans) as the 22nd Missouri Historic Site. These historic properties are now open to the public at all times.

The paintings of Anna and Clarence Hesse hang in literally hundreds of homes, and their church is enriched by stained glass windows made by the Hesses. The "Pageants" (nine of them), once regularly featured at the early annual Maifests, were all written and directed by Anna. All were based on episodes of authentic history of the town.

Some achievement for a simple country gal!

Turn the page

to meet Missouri's

forgotten *dog*

who made history

". . . was known to correctly predict sports and political outcomes"

Jim the Wonder Dog
Keen Canine Canniness

Though most dog owners claim to have the smartest, most clever and intelligent dogs on the face of the earth, one dog in Missouri history rises above the lot. Jim, the Wonder Dog, could do more than shake a mangy paw, beg for leftovers and roll over and play dead for his owner.

Jim, born in 1925, was given to Sam VanArsdale of West Plains, Missouri, as a gift. Jim came from a long line of well-known field dogs. As Sam tried to train Jim to fetch feathered quarry, he soon realized Jim's astute intellect was far beyond that of most fire-hydrant-sniffing canines.

Jim was quick to carry out any verbal (or even written) commands that Sam offered. When told to point out a hickory, oak or walnut tree, he always pointed out the correct one.

He would amaze nonbelievers by picking out cars by color, make or license plate number as they commanded (even when the car was cleverly parked three blocks away).

Jim even seemed able to read people's minds and was known to correctly predict sports and political outcomes.

Jim would accompany Sam to the cigar shop every week, where Sam would say "O.K. Jim, pick out my favorite cigars" at which point Jim would point them out. One day, the shop keeper moved the cigars to the opposite wall just to test ole Jim.

The next week, as Sam gave the familiar command to his dog, Jim smoked the merchant by unblinkingly pointing out Sam's favorite stogies on the opposite wall.

Sam toured throughout the state with the Wonder Dog exhibiting his amazing talents. The authenticity of Jim's keen canine canniness was attested to by many, including college professors who reported that Jim seemed to respond equally well to commands in Italian, French, German, Spanish and even Greek.

When Jim died in 1937, the VanArsdales requested that Jim be allowed to join their beloved departed in the Marshall Cemetery. Their dog plot plea was denied, however, and Jim was buried just outside the gate of the Ridge Park Cemetery in Marshall. In an ironic twist, the cemetery has grown to encompass the area where Jim now lies.

A Missouri classic entitled *Jim, the Wonder Dog* by Clarence Dewey Mitchell, originally published in 1942, is a great read including many of Jim's adventures and how he quickly won the praise of even ardent skeptics. The book is even written from Jim's point of view.

“The attic of his home in Bethel was given over to plants that he, alone, tended”

Wilhelm Keil
Commune Leader, Saint or Mad Mystic?

Wilhelm Keil, founder of the Bethel Colony in Shelby County: was he the saint some saw, benevolent and wise, or the rigid tyrant others wrote of? Did he, as some whispered, practice the black arts when he wasn't preparing his good sermons?

We'll never know. We can only review what's been written about him and handed down word-of-mouth. One indisputable fact is that in 1844, Keil created one of the most successful communes in our nation's history. It functioned productively for 35 years, then disbanded in orderly fashion, with its sizeable assets fairly divided.

Bethel's uniqueness was its apparent freedom, the only control seemingly Keil's keeping consciences awake by example and by preaching about the Golden Rule, serving others gladly, doing one's duty and fighting the urge for luxury. Though this was a Christian community, church attendance was optional and no acceptance of certain creeds was demanded. No singular dress was worn and no peculiar customs were followed. Family life was not manipulated nor the young systematically indoctrinated. Work was unassigned, done rather on a basis of interest, ability and what most needed to be done at any given time.

For their labor, members received home, furnishings and fuel, medicines, clothing, food from common stores and from the animals and garden plots given to each family. Members could profit individually from spare-time pursuits and interact as they chose with neighbors "outside." Non-members regularly shopped at Bethel or attended services in its large and lovely church. Planned festivities were frequent, including the Harvestfest beloved of Germans.

Accomplishments of the colony were impressive. Gloves and shoes made there sold readily outside, and Bethel's whiskey was shipped to eager markets all over the country. Wool from the colony's huge flock of sheep was much respected and the Bethel band, in natty uniforms, was considered a jewel of the region.

The main flaw noted in Keil was his indifference to higher education. The colony's school taught only the basics. He said going to college through individual or family efforts was fine, but it would be unfair to use colony resources for the education of people who might not come back to share their learning.

Keil kept a firm grip, serving as secretary and treasurer as well as minister, but a board of trustees audited his books regularly and all sources say nobody ever doubted his honesty. Trustees and colonists helped make all important decisions.

Still, rumors about Keil persisted. He was a Prussian, born in 1811, the poorly educated son of a tailor. He was described as handsome in his youth, an excellent worker. Strong religious seekings led him to dabble in the occult as well as established denominations. Some said that Keil brought to this country occult books and powerful knowledge. The attic of his home at Bethel was given over to plants that he, alone, tended.

During the religious fervor of the 1830s, Keil developed a following of immigrants willing to pool their cash to buy land. They invested $30,802.75 in a new Missouri county, their writings say, on "a beautiful tableland on the banks of the North River." Their original purchase was four sections, 2,460 acres, and in only ten years they had added almost twice as much again. Bethel Colony's population grew to about 1,000.

Charles Nordhoff visited Bethel and described it in his book, *The Communistic Societies of the United States.* He said that, though the colony had a pharmacist, Keil also treated Bethelites with a combination of his mysterious medicines and psychological understandings far ahead of his time. It was said that people would go to him incapable of working and would come away looking and feeling like new, or that they made startling recovery in a time span predicted by Keil.

Much was written of the leader's blue eyes, "bold and searching," in one writer's words, "which seemed to penetrate to the heart and soul of whomever he spoke with, conveying infinite love and concern, drawing forth unquestioning devotion and obedience." Nordhoff implied that Keil might have had his people on drugs to make them hyper for work and lethargic when that was, in his opinion, best. The pharmacy held herbal remedies enough for several times the number of people living at Bethel.

Adolph E. Schroeder, a retired professor of German American studies at the University of Missouri-Columbia, is probably the state's best authority on Keil and Bethel. He believes there was nothing sinister about the man; he was just highly charismatic, blessed with a strong personality and great leadership skills, "one who could operate almost as a dictator and make everyone like it." Dr. Schroeder adds that German immigrants were usually hardworking and quiet, accustomed to strong leadership and reassured by it.

Lucille Bower, a Bethel resident interviewed in 1987 for *Rural Missouri,* said there were stories of Keil's abusing confidences given him as counselor, and that his favorite tactic was making people feel that any misfortune was their own fault. He may have regretted this in later life when four of his children died of smallpox within one month, two of them on a single day.

An earlier loss in 1855 had already brought Keil's eccentricity into full play, when he had decided to set up a duplicate colony in the West. While Bethel planned the trip, Keil's son Willie died. This young man had intended to drive the leading wagon, so Keil had him put into an iron coffin with viewing window (some sources said preserved with Bethel whiskey) and hauled all the way to Oregon.

This often caused hardship but proved a protection to the party. Two or three times Keil forged on despite warnings about hostile Indians and wrote back to Bethel "I had all power over the Indians. I could do with them as I desired." In reality, it seemed, some tribes, having heard about Willie, stayed away, horrified that a father could be so cruel as to deny a son burial at home. Others, because the Bethelites sang as they traveled, respected the party as a religious pilgrimage.

Keil met all problems with confidence. He wrote that in the desert, where they lost many animals, he saw no alternative but "to ride ahead of the train, from sunrise to sunset, cursing and abjuring these places of Hell and death." Thus, he wrote with satisfaction, he brought through "every soul and every wagon . . . and the devil has been put to shame forever by me!"

Making this trip without even one human death was, indeed, an achievement.

The new colony settled at what is now Aurora, Oregon, and proved successful, but Keil died suddenly on December 30, 1877. Within two years of his death, Bethel's residents had dissolved the old colony, but most of them stayed on, living as they had before, just adopting a few more comfortable and worldly ways.

Keil's memory is kept alive in the historical materials and events offered at Bethel, which went on the National Registry of Historic Places in 1970. Its 150 remaining residents arrange several annual public entertainments that blend the town's past and present. These renew our curiosity about the remarkable man who put it all there. And whether we see him as saint or mad mystic, Wilhelm Keil did prove that people can live harmoniously and comfortably with pooled resources.

The "real Whig leader of Missouri"

Abiel Leonard
Frontier Lawyer

On first glance, all would agree that Abiel Leonard had no chance for success as a frontier lawyer. He scarcely met the standard for rugged manhood. With a face everyone considered homely, he was said to have fainted after being attacked, and to have "taken to his bed" when a favorite horse died. Leonard's success in Missouri's Little Dixie was further hindered by his penniless beginnings as a Unionist among ardent Rebels (many of them rich and powerful) and by his health problems, which sapped his energy and often incapacitated him.

However, this man — who had never fired a pistol before — challenged one attacker to a duel and killed him, and eventually accumulated 60,000 acres of land and the unofficial national title "real Whig leader of Missouri." As a supreme court judge, he helped set Missouri's infant code of law onto a fair and temperate course.

Some chronology: Abiel (pronounced Uh Bile) Leonard was born in Vermont in 1797, a descendant of Welsh immigrants. His American forebears included legislators, clergymen and jurists. Abiel's own father was a captain in the American Army and commander of Fort Niagara. Once, in his unauthorized absence, British forces attacked Niagara and captured more than 300 soldiers. Nathaniel Leonard lost his command and his family suffered permanent social and financial embarrassment.

Abiel's Dartmouth College days being shortened by his father's actions, he read law in New York state and in his early 20s headed west, landing at St. Louis in 1818 or 1819, walking on to Rocheport, his belongings in a bundle on a stick. Unable to get law clients there, he went to Boonville, passed the county bar and opened an office.

The "unusual and interesting personality," one writer describes, "which made people like Leonard and remember him" flowered there. Leonard proved an effective speaker, his voice surprisingly powerful, his black eyes compelling. In three years, his practice included several counties, and in 1824 Leonard was chosen circuit attorney.

This was the year of his duel, and the story told by historians is: Taylor Berry, prosperous land developer and Franklin postmaster, was prosecuted by Leonard, and though he was acquitted something enraged Berry. He attacked Leonard with a large whip. Leonard faced Berry on Wolf Island in the Mississippi near New Madrid on August 31 or September 1, 1824. His shot to the chest felled Berry immediately, but he lived until

September 22. Leonard was fined $150, disbarred and stripped of his civic rights, but his popularity was such that a petition for restoration was granted on December 24 of the same year. His giving up prosecution, which could have been very profitable, must indicate something of his feelings.

A decade later, having gained great respect among important Missourians, Leonard was appointed to the Missouri supreme court. Some of Leonard's clients were big names at the time — Thomas Hart Benton, for one, when he was sued for debt. Leonard brought the Mormon plea for civic protection and represented merchants engaged in Santa Fe Trail trade.

A number of prominent people retained Leonard as private counselor. His law office attracted readers fated for future importance, among them James Rollins, remembered as "Father of the University," and W. F. Switzler, owner editor of a powerful newspaper.

Two samples of laws Leonard wrote while in the state supreme court:

. . . far ahead of his time, Leonard decreed that married women should have control of any money or property belonging to them alone, just as they would if they were "a femme sole." (Few states were so liberal.)

. . . Leonard wrote that to ensure equal treatment for all, a code of law should have as many fixed rules as possible. "Too much is left up to the discretion of the judge," he said.

Leonard's abilities and success gave him entry to an elite group of politicians that included Rollins, Switzler, the artist George Caleb Bingham, and Dr. William Jewell. Some of Leonard's most satisfying moments must have come on June 18-20, 1840, when he was referred to as leader of the nation's biggest Whig convention. This was held in Rocheport to elect a presidential candidate in the year of William Henry Harrison and the famous slogan "Tippecanoe and Tyler too." Missouri's population of 400,000 included 23,000 Whigs and several thousand of those surely gave Rocheport as much color as ever was seen in all of its colorful history.

Arriving by foot, horseback, carriage and riverboat, the delegates created a tent city and marched in a mile-long parade with bands and banners. Impassioned orators rotating among four platforms included Leonard, Bingham, Rollins, Switzler and their prominent colleagues.

Harrison won the election, only to die a month after inauguration and Tyler performed much differently than the Whigs had expected, but Leonard's reputation did not change. Prewar stirrings brought him to the conviction that a gradual, peaceful way must be found to end slavery. Several wealthy Missourians were freeing a few slaves at a time as they could be prepared to make their own living. These Whigs were for state's rights but against secession and, when war came, served Lincoln. Leonard wrote in a letter, "I regret that in the hour of my country's need, I have no strength of body to offer in her aid."

Leonard's work, requiring frequent travel, made him an absentee father, but he kept warm contact with his seven children by Jeanette Reeves, daughter of Col. Benjamin H. Reeves, former Lt. Governor of Missouri. He insisted on regular letters from all and filed these as carefully as he did his business papers. Leonard's replies showed affection for his children and determined educational input. For instance, with his eldest son, Reeves, he discussed the achievements of Benton, one of Missouri's first U.S. senators. He said these came less from rare talent than from persistent effort, a tactic available to all. He also said "I shall not feel I have lived to no purpose when I leave behind such a son as you. God bless you and preserve you."

Some might have enjoyed seeing Leonard's land speculations fail until his credit was withdrawn, but after his 1863 death, war changed land values and his mortgaged holdings were readily liquidated. Leonard's land made his heirs more than comfortable. Had he lived another decade, he would have been revered as an astute investor.

Abiel Leonard's home, Oakwood, originally on 500 acres near Fayette, still stands — a private dwelling carefully preserved, looking much as *The WPA Guide to 1930s Missouri* describes: "two story red brick with one story white wood portico and fanlighted entrance, original brick slave cabins behind." It is not open to the public. Leonard would never have seen the mansion at nearby Ravenswood, built by his nephew in 1880, but earlier he was often at the farm, seeing vistas much the same as we see today.

Visitors there should perhaps think a little of the sickly young man who overcame so many disadvantages to make a life both useful to others and satisfying to himself. And, should we ever face a Missouri judge, we may need to thank Abiel Leonard for all his efforts to make our laws just and reasonable.

"he sat down with some of the same cronies who had robbed him the fall before . . ."

William Rodney Massie
A Riverboat Captain, Not a Gambler

When it comes to describing old-time pilots on the Missouri River, it's best to let those who were there tell the story. Capt. Wm. L. Heckmann Jr. (Steamboat Bill), Dr. E. B. Trail and an unidentified St. Louis, Missouri, newspaper obituary writer are the source of this story.

Captain William Rodney Massie was a Mountain Pilot. The upper reaches of the Missouri River are about 1,600 miles long, from where it tumbles over the great falls above Fort Benton, Montana, to Kansas City, Missouri. When you can steamboat those waters, you're known as a Mountain Pilot, and there is no other stretch of river of this length in the known world where as much skill is needed to get a boat up and down the river as there is right here. This river will change its channel while you eat your breakfast. Anyone who can pilot a boat successfully here can qualify as a first-class pilot on any river in the world.

Born in 1831 and raised about two miles east of Hermann on the Missouri River, young Bill Massie and his older brother John took to the water as youngsters and never left it. In 1845, the steamer *Big Hatchie* blew up while leaving the Hermann wharf, maiming and killing many of the crew and passengers. John and Bill Massie, coming upriver in a skiff, helped save many of these unfortunate people and were the first on board the burning wreck. Some 40 of these people, mostly crew members and immigrants going out west to seek a new home, are buried in a single unmarked grave in the Hermann cemetery. An obelisk, erected in the cemetery by the Brush and Palette Club, stands in mute testimony to those who lost their lives. Seeing this disaster in no way discouraged the Massie boys from following a career on the steamboats.

Bill Massie first served in 1846 on the steamer *Bertrand* — the same steamer whose remains are on display at the museum at DeSoto Bend on the Missouri, north of Council Bluffs, Iowa. He often carried Col. William F. Cody, famous as Buffalo Bill, to the forts on the Missouri. The two formed a lifelong friendship.

Massie came in contact with the Quantrell-James-Younger guerilla band in 1862 while he was pilot on the *Fannie Ogden*. The boat was lying close to the bank and some of the gang pulled guns on the crew. However, the gang did not molest the boat.

In 1866, when piloting the steamer *Cora,* owned by Capt. Kinney, he received a monthly salary of $2,500. At a later date this was exceeded, for on one trip, when there was a valuable cargo and more than 200 passengers aboard, he received $1,000 a day, it is said, for taking the *Cora* safely into port.

Capt. Massie, while he owned several fine boats outright and was master of many more, was at heart just a pilot. He made more trips as a pilot from St. Louis to Fort Benton then any other man (with the possible exception of Capt. Joe LaBarge). When we consider that this same man piloted wooden steamboats for 60 years and only sank one boat, the steamer *Montana,* one can imagine the skill of this navigator.

His fame as a pilot was such that boats with less experienced pilots, when coming back to St. Louis on the tail end of the June rise, would wait until Massie's boat started home. Then both the owners and the pilots of these boats would pay him so they could follow his boat out to St. Louis. People often wondered why, when they would see six or eight boats coming down the river, one right behind the other.

Capt. Massie loved the great American game of poker, either straight or stud proper, for he could lose just about as much in either game. He always thought he was a great player; but he was honest, and honesty in his heyday on a steamboat lost you money, and much more, among the card sharks in St. Louis.

He loved to tell a story on himself about his poker playing. He got paid something close to $7,000 one morning for a round trip to the mountains. After a late breakfast he started up town, but he could not pass one of his favorite taverns, which had a sign hanging inside saying "Fools Do Not Linger Here."

He sat down with some of the same cronies who had robbed him the fall before. He started a big game at 9 a.m. and at 5 p.m. he got up, flat broke. When he got out on the pavement he found a loose dime in his pocket. He said to himself, "I will flip it and if tails come up I will get a shot of tanglefoot and if heads come up it will be a roll and a cup of coffee." Up it went in the air, but instead of falling on the pavement, it fell in one of the pavement grates for which downtown St. Louis was famous. He stepped aside to scrape his cash out of the grate and when he saw that dime again it looked as big as a wagon wheel, he was so desperate for loose change.

Massie's gambling instincts caused him to leave his boat and head for the gold fields. When he joined the Black Hills gold rush he was sitting in a game of poker with "Wild Bill" Hickok when that mighty man fell dead with a bullet in his back. "Billy the Kid" also wanted to learn the river under Capt. Massie, but he did not have the money a man needed in those days to get a cub's berth, so he went to shooting men. He soon had to get the stock on his rifle lengthened to make room for more notches.

Capt. Massie sank just one boat, the big steamer *Montana.* Coming upstream with a tow he hit the bridge peer of the St. Charles Wabash Bridge. Later, Capt. John Gonsollis sank *Dacotah* on a big stump, but she was raised, her owners losing a season's profit. Capt. Massie said surely Gonsollis did not sink the *Dacotah* on an obstruction as prominent as that stump. Gonsollis retorted that the stump was not as prominent as the St. Charles bridge where Massie sunk the *Montana.*

Massie never retired. The call of the freshwater was so strong he never denied his desire to be on board the boats. Not until the fall before his death did he come home to his family in St. Louis. He left a wife and six children to mourn his passing.

"legions of trail buffs retraced the route . . ."

Merrill Mattes

Blazing Trails through Pen and Ink

Merril Mattes, perhaps the country's preeminent overland trails scholar, helped blaze America's great trails straight into the class room, the textbook and America's conscience.

Mattes's book *Great Platte River Road* (1969) brought the Oregon Trails saga to thousands of readers. Mattes evaluated more than 2,000 original overland diaries and journals in *Platte River Road Narratives* (1988), now considered the basic research manual by modern-day trails scholars.

But Mattes's greatest legacy may be the grip that the overland trails story holds on the imagination of Americans today. In 1993, upon the 150th anniversary of the Oregon Trail, legions of trails buffs retraced the route on horseback, on bicycle, in replica covered wagons and on foot.

"I'm glad that he lived to see this new surge of interest in the westward trails," said John Mark Lumbertson, director of the National Frontier Trails Center in Independence. "That really did delight him."

In 1991, Mattes donated his working library to the trails center. Today the Merrill J. Mattes Research Library is considered the largest such public library in the country devoted to the American overland trail experience. In 1993, Mattes augmented the collection by approving the transfer from the Nebraska State Historical Society of about 50 cubic feet of his own manuscripts, maps and photographs.

Mattes, who was born in the Chicago area, was a 1927 graduate of Central High School in Kansas City. He spent three years working part-time in the clippings library of the *Kansas City Star*. After earning degrees in history, from the University of Missouri in 1931, and English literature, from the University of Kansas in 1933, he worked as a market reporter for the Kansas City Stockyards Company.

In 1935 he became a ranger for the National Park Service and the first salaried superintendent of Scotts Bluff National Monument in western Nebraska — one of the great landmarks along the Oregon Trail.

Mattes retired in 1975 after 40 years as a park service historian and preservationist. Over the years he published about 50 trails articles in quarterly journals, as well as about 200 book reviews on trails history. The topic, he told a reporter in 1988, had been well worth his time and effort.

"It's one of the few major episodes in our history that makes us unique as a nation," he said. "It consolidated the United States of America, and I don't think it's sufficiently appreciated."

"... haranguing against the devil's brew and busting up saloons ..."

Carry A. Nation
Keg Smashin' Pioneer Abolitionist

With the fury of an avenging angel, Carry A. Nation disembarked from railroad platforms in small Midwestern towns in the early 1900s, haranguing against the devil's brew and busting up saloons with her trademark chopper. In usually serene places like Enterprise and Holt in Kansas, windows, tables, chairs, counters, bottles and tap lines fell to pieces beneath the hammer blows of her infamous hatchet. Local authorities were called in to restore the peace and toss her behind bars.

Nation's ritual purifications — honored by her persecutors with showers of eggs, rotten produce, fists and whips — were publicly disavowed at first even by her fellow crusaders in the Women's Christian Temperance Union. (They later awarded her a gold medal as the bravest woman in Kansas.) Though she intended to carry on until no drink stronger than water could be bought or sold anywhere in the nation, all her smashing and bashing of other people's property got her in jake with the law, and she ended up lecturing and hawking souvenir hatchets to finance her legal expenses.

As a girl Nation lived near Belton, Missouri. She moved to Kansas City, and then, with her first husband, to Holden, Missouri. After spending her life attempting to <u>carry</u> <u>a</u> <u>nation</u> toward sobriety, she ended up back in Belton, where her hatchet swings no more.

"she helped sell socialism in the heart of America . . ."

Kate Richards O'Hare
First Lady of Socialism

A writer, political reformer and spellbinding speaker, O'Hare helped sell socialism in the heart of America. Crisscrossing the country, she organized and agitated among farmers, factory workers and miners and rose to the top ranks of the Socialist party, winning a seat on its national executive committee and serving a stint as the party's international secretary.

In 1912, O'Hare and her husband Frank moved to St. Louis, accepting an invitation to join the editorial staff of the *National Rip-Saw*, a monthly socialist newspaper, featuring lurid exposes and hard-hitting editorials. O'Hare wrote a popular column for the paper, and she and her husband helped boost the *Rip-Saw*'s paid circulation to about 150,000, making it the second-largest socialist newspaper in the country. In 1916, she became a candidate to represent Missouri in the U.S. Senate, the first woman ever to seek election to that body.

After O'Hare spoke on July 29, 1917, in Bowman, North Dakota, she was arrested on the charge of intending to interfere with the national war effort, a criminal offense under the federal Espionage Act.

O'Hare was sentenced to five years in the Missouri Penitentiary and began serving her time in April 1919. Prison conditions appalled O'Hare, and she used her fame and outside contacts to get the cell block painted, have showers installed and ensure that the women prisoners got warm meals. But her socialist sensibilities were most offended by the contract labor system, under which the women prisoners spent nine hours a day sewing clothes for a manufacturing company.

O'Hare's sentence was commuted by President Woodrow Wilson on May 29, 1920, and she made prison reform the primary focus of her remaining years.

". . . she descended into batty darkness by the light of candles . . ."

Luella Owen
Dainty Aristocratic Spelunker

Luella Owen slipped out of her gilded cage, suited up in a divided skirt that was probably scandalously short (it touched her boot tops!) and proceeded to seek her pleasures underground.

Luelle Owen's curiosity exposed her to a side of St. Joseph, Missouri, that had been overlooked by her white, upper-crust peers. Women of Owen's generation and breeding, their spheres of action limited to the parlor and drawing room, typically aspired only to marry well. Owen, by contrast, aspired to investigate underground geology.

As Missouri's first notable cave woman, or spelunker, she descended into batty darkness by the light of candles and white magnesium ribbon and groped her way toward an understanding of cave geology.

Through her experiences, Owen became a teacher and cave conservationist. She spoke out to preserve the caves from being stripped by their owners, and her explorations were the basis for her lively book *Cave Regions of the Ozarks and Black Hills* (1898), for many years the standard work on Missouri caves.

Owen's fame as a geologist rested primarily on her study of loess soil. This so-called sugar dirt, visible and abundant in the excavations in and around St. Joseph, was the subject of a long-standing debate in geological circles. In her scholarly writing, Owen supported the theory that loess had been deposited by glacial action rather than by wind. Her work on the subject was internationally known.

Owen was one of three remarkable, independently wealthy sisters (see Mary Alicia Owen, next profile) who alternated traveling in pursuit of their careers with staying at home in St. Joseph to care for their sick mother. Despite the social pressures of their upper-class milieu, none of the three married, and they lived quite happily.

"she feared that the knowledge of voodoo symbols . . . could be misused . . ."

Mary Alicia Owen
Voodoo Expert and Woman Folklorist

Fueled by burning curiosity, Mary Owen, the oldest of several remarkable sisters from St. Joseph, Missouri (see also Luella Owen), collected and published folk tales, wrote novels and became a recognized authority on folklore.

Her interest in ethnicity led her to spend much time in St. Joseph with local blacks, Indians, and the Welsh, Irish and German immigrants. She frequently visited the Sac Indians, who adopted her as a member of the tribe. By the time she reached adulthood, the unquenchably curious child who had so nagged her "aunties" for stories was so proficient at cross-cultural interviewing that she wrote one of the most important 19th-century books on black American folklore and even gained access to the virtually impenetrable world of black voodoo.

Owen was born on January 29, 1850, in St. Joseph. Educated at home by her mother and at local public schools, she spent a year at Vassar College from 1868 to 1869. Back at home, she began to write for newspapers and magazines under the pen name Julia Scott, contributing a column on local settlers to the *St. Joseph Saturday Democrat* and writing short stories for magazines.

Her horizons widened after reading Charles Godfrey Leland's book *Algonquin Legends of New England.* Owen recognized Leland's stories as being similar to the ones she'd heard around St. Joseph. Owen wrote Leland, sending him samples of the folk tales she had gathered. The initial exchange of letters between the two started a personal and professional correspondence that lasted throughout their lives. Leland became Owen's closest friend and her mentor and encouraged Owen to travel to London to present a paper at the 1891 Folklore Congress and to publish her material in a book.

In 1893, with Leland's help, Owen's first book of folklore was published by T. Fisher Unwin in London. The book, *Old Rabbit the Voodoo and Other Sorcerers*, was a collection of tales, written in dialect, that Owen had gathered from Missouri blacks.

Though Leland urged her to translate the tales for her white audience, Owen instead rendered the dialect she'd heard as faithfully as possible. Here, from one of the tales, is a snatch of dialogue between an old Woodpecker and a young Woodpecker that may help explain Leland's initial concerns with usage:

"[Young Woodpecker]: 'Looky hyeah at my laig!'

Old Woodpeckeh look, look long time an' say nuttin.

Den he cuss.

Den he ax, 'Who done dat?'

'Dat boy down in de holler.'

'Wut he done dat foh?'

'Foh nuttin. I ain't tetch 'im. I ain't ez much az sen' my shadder cross 'cross 'im.'

'Nemmine! Nemmine! Des wait, my child, twell yo' daddy mek de 'quaintance ob dat boy.'

'Fix my laig fust , daddy.'

'Dat wut I gwine ter do, my son.'

Den Ole Woodpeckeh fix that laig up good ez new."

Owen's narratives employed techniques similar to those used by her famous contemporary, Joel Chandler Harris, author of the Uncle Remus stories. Like Harris, Owen selected talking animal stories from the lore she had gathered and used several black women as narrators to tell the tales. These so-called "aunties" included Aunt Jinny, an authority on natural healing; jolly Aunt Emily, pudgy as a newborn child; oily Aunt Mary, who had entertained ghosts; and satanic Aunt Mymee, who considered herself the daughter of the devil.

At the urging of Leland, Owen next began work on a study of voodoo magic, a difficult subject few scholars had touched. Though a middle-aged, properly raised white woman on alien turf, Owen was able to make headway. Equipped with material she had already collected, assisted by her informants in St. Joseph's black community, she interviewed important voodoos, such as King Alexander, when they visited St. Joseph. She even traveled to Cuba to do some fact-finding.

Working upstairs in the family house by morning, helping her sisters care for their widowed mother and entertaining guests in the parlor in the late afternoons, Owen steadily advanced her project. In 1894, after two years' work, however, she stalled and withheld her manuscript for years, keeping the work under lock and key.

Having witnessed firsthand the chilling fear that voodoo practitioners could strike in their victims, Owen apparently feared that the knowledge of voodoo symbols and rituals she was imparting could be misused by irresponsible readers. Twenty years later, her grand-niece casually mentioned her own interest in voodoo. Owen responded that she had written a book on the subject but later burned the manuscript, page by page, in the household fireplace.

Though her magnum opus was gone, Owen did incorporate her knowledge of voodoo into her fiction. One of the main characters to appear in her 1896 novel, *The Daughter of Alouette*, was Queen Ahola, an evil voodoo priestess who tries to poison with racial hate a half-breed girl named Tamminika. The priestess — dressed in robes, surrounded by shrines, symbols painted on her fingernails — could just as well have appeared in a work of nonfiction.

Owen's writing didn't interfere with her other passion. She continued her cross-cultural work and became recognized as an authority on folklore. When the Missouri Folklore Society was established in 1906, she was among the charter members. As she turned 50, Owen, now growing plump and matronly, embarked on a new project — collecting and preserving the Indian lore of northwest Missouri, fast disappearing as Indians were exiled to reservations or assimilated into the larger culture. Indian burial grounds that had existed in Owen's youth were now covered by municipal buildings.

Owen started making regular trips to the camps of the Musquakie tribes, which had been resettled in Brown and Doniphan Counties in Kansas. Though as a woman she was not permitted to speak with the men of the tribe, she spent her time in conversation with the squaws, eliciting information about customs and ceremonies that were falling into disuse. Owen's first paper on Musquakie folklore was presented at a meeting of the British Folk-Lore Congress in Toronto in 1897.

Owen's paper drew an enthusiastic response. Officers of the British Folk-Lore Society asked her to expand it into a book. Six years later, in 1904, the society published Owen's *Folklore of the Musquakie Indians of North America*, which included a catalogue of the Musquakie artifact and beadwork collection that Owen donated to the society. The book brought congratulations from Leland and educated readers in the United States and England.

At the same time, Owen was busy with other projects. In 1900 she wrote an article on Missouri lore for the *Encyclopedia of the History of Missouri,* and in addition to her work on the Musquakie she had two books — *Oracles and Witches* (1904) and *Sacred Council Hills* (1907) — published by the British Folk-Lore Society. In 1909, she was elected president of the Missouri Folklore Society, holding that office until her death in 1934.

"Riley's famous four-crunch lunch"

Charles Valentine Riley
Plagued by Bugs His Whole Life

Charles Valentine Riley, born September 18, 1843, in London, England, lacked a formal education in entomology, but he became one of the foremost students of insect life in 19th-century America. His nine-volume work, *Noxious, Beneficial and Other Insects of the State of Missouri,* was viewed as a classic in its field and brought him almost immediate recognition. Prized by farmers and scientists alike, Riley's reports combined insight and accuracy with flights of whimsy and rapture.

Here is Riley in a playful mood, dimming the lights and lifting the curtain on one of his research subjects, a caterpillar called the raspberry geometer *(Aplodes rubivora):* "The lovers of those most exquisite fruits, the Raspberry and the Blackberry, are often greatly disgusted by the discovery of the fact that instead of the delicious berry which they expected to enjoy, they are munching the small caterpillar now under consideration."

Riley left Europe at age 17, after studying in France and Germany. He settled on a farm outside Chicago and began contributing articles to the *Prairie Farmer*, an agricultural journal. Eventually the *Prairie Farmer* hired him as a reporter, artist and entomology editor.

If Riley's life were in a play, it would be staged in three acts. Only 25 when, in 1868, he was appointed Missouri's first entomologist, he soon made a name for himself. His first triumph came in 1871. At the invitation of the French government Riley crossed the Atlantic and inspected France's ailing grape crop, the wellspring of its prized wines. The Professor, as he later came to be known, diagnosed the problem as an infestation of an American plant louse called grape *Phylloxera.* He prescribed disease-resistant American vines as one possible cure. His suggestion not only helped restore millions of acres of French vines that had wilted and died, it provided business for several Missouri viniculturists, who shipped millions of cuttings to France. For his work, the French government awarded Riley a gold medal.

Riley, paid a meager $2,500 a year and provided with no furniture, equipment or assistants for his St. Louis office, continued his pioneering work despite the lack of appreciation from Missouri politicians. When clouds of grasshoppers invaded Missouri in 1874, laying eggs thick enough to whiten the surface of plowed ground, the official response from the state's chief executive, Gov. Charles Henry Hardin, was an attempt to appease the God or gods who had cooked up the plague. In his famous "Grasshopper Proclamation," Hardin set aside June 3 as an official day of fasting and prayer. The state legislature meanwhile put a bounty of $5 a bushel on grasshopper eggs. Riley, ever the scientist, studied the invasion. He gathered historical information on grasshopper plagues in the Midwest and mapped their extent.

After the grasshopper eggs hatched in the spring of 1875 and the plague struck with full force in western Missouri, Riley suggested that rather than go hungry the farmers eat the insects. The idea was ridiculed,

Riley made his point by serving a famous four-course meal. The menu, which consisted of locust soup, baked locusts, locust cakes, locusts with honey and just plain locusts, apparently pleased his guests.

though Riley tried to promote locusts as a flavorful alternative to meat and potatoes. To introduce his friends to the delicacy, he carried around with him a small box of fried grasshoppers. At the Eads House in Warrensburg Riley made his point by serving a famous four-course meal. The menu, which consisted of locust soup, baked locusts, locust cakes, locusts with honey and just plain locusts, apparently pleased his guests.

Riley's response to the plague helped solidify his reputation and demonstrate the potential value of scientific pest control. Riley turned his studies of the plague into a book on grasshoppers, and he pressed for federal laws to combat the pests. In 1877, U.S. Congress created a three-member entomological commission to study the ravages of the Rocky Mountain Locust, and Riley, then 34, was made chairman. Soon after, Riley accepted an offer to become entomologist of the U.S. Bureau of Agriculture.

Nine months after he took office, Riley resigned, having fallen into disfavor with his boss, the Commissioner of Agriculture. In March 1881, with a change in administration, Riley returned to his post as chief entomologist at the U.S. Commission of Agriculture and was instrumental in saving the California citrus industry from the Cottony Cushion Scale.

By 1883, the scale had done so much damage to California orchards that state officials appointed a special committee to plot its destruction. Riley sent two men, D. W. Coquillett and Albert Koebele, to Los Angeles and Alameda to investigate the situation. Despite repeated attempts to eradicate the tenacious scale with gases and washes of various kinds, the scale kept its foothold in the orchards.

Working out of Washington, D.C., Riley traced the insect to Australia. He asked an Australian scientist, Fraser H. Crawford, to check whether the Cottony Cushion Scale was controlled by any natural predators in its native land. Circumventing Congress, which refused his requests for money for a trip to Australia, Riley approached the Secretary of State and obtained permission to send two Department of Agriculture agents to Australia as part of a commission being created to represent the United States at the Melbourne Exposition.

Arriving in Australia in 1888, field agent Albert Koebele teamed up with Fraser H. Crawford. On October 15 in North Adelaide, Koebele discovered the larva of a ladybird beetle feeding on one of the scale insects. Koebele recognized the importance of his find and began sending live specimens to Coquillet in Los Angeles. By late January 1889, Coquillet had received 129 specimens of the beetle. He placed them under a tent on an orange tree infested by the scale insect. The beetles, allowed to breed freely, devoured the scale insects in the experimental area. They were then set free in the surrounding orchard and distributed to orchards throughout the state.

By 1892, California's citrus orchards were virtually rid of the Cottony Cushion Scale. Riley's efforts had helped save the California citrus industry millions of dollars at the cost of little more than $1,500 to the agriculture department.

Riley resigned from the agriculture department in 1894 and became honorary curator of the Department of Insects at the U.S. National Museum. His personal collection of 115,000 mounted insects, numbering 15,000 species, was donated to the museum, and it became the core of one of the nation's largest insect collections. A year later, on September 15, 1895, he died of head injuries sustained in a bicycle accident.

". . . On his head is a smaller man, also balanced on one foot . . ."

James Robinson
World Champion Bareback Rider

It is difficult to think of anything being done on a horse's back that was not accomplished by James Robinson." This is how a circus historian described a man who lived for several decades on an elaborate farm he established near Mexico, Missouri. Accepted as the world's champion bareback rider, Robinson spent part of each year touring the world with his act, and the other months enjoying Audrain County's natural beauties and warm atmosphere.

In the 1860s, Robinson's performances earned him $50,000 a year, as well as a valuable collection of silver, crystal and jeweled souvenirs given to him by the adoring royalty he perfomed for. Queen Victoria's offering was a diamond stickpin designed exclusively for him. Robinson toured Europe four times and was said to have ridden in almost every country of the world.

Born James Michael Fitzgerald in Boston, Massachusetts, in 1835, Robinson was orphaned at the age of six. He was taken to a monastery that his father had endowed, with the understanding that his son was to be reared there and educated for the priesthood. At eight, James escaped by climbing over the wall and took refuge in a circus wagon.

When discovered, he presented himself as a homeless waif who did not know his last name. The owner of the circus took him into his family and reared him as his own. Preparing the boy for a circus career, he began with trapeze work but soon saw that James liked horses better.

Young Robinson must have been a talented observer and determined to study, because at only 22, he went to compete in a circus championship in Washington, D.C. Robinson's reputation was such that only one other person showed up to compete. His name was John Glenroy, the first and only rider to do somersaults on horseback. In preparation for meeting him, young Robinson worked out a routine more graceful and far more demanding than Glenroy's.

He learned to do somersaults in a series, four per circuit of the ring, and he did them both forward and backward. Up to that time, nobody had somersaulted forward on a horse.

Whether or not everyone in the world considered this a legitimate championship win, the title gave Robinson entry to the best and biggest circuses. When he performed in Havana, Cuba, citizens there presented him with an impressive gold and diamond championship belt. Over the years, he defended this many times, usually against riders much younger than himself.

In 1873, at 38, Robinson was signed on as a star attraction of the Great Eastern Circus, one of the most important of the era. That may also be the year he first saw Mexico, Missouri, and found it a dream fulfilled. He had never before known a friendly small-town atmosphere and he, who had seen the world but never found a home, found Audrain's prairie terrain totally satisfying. Robinson also was looking for safety and peace. His highly publicized earnings and rich gifts had made him a frequent target of robbery attempts. He said he'd killed two men in self-defense. Between tours, Mexico gave him refuge from all that.

Robinson bought 1,100 acres and established a profitable livestock operation as well as a place to train new horses. *The History of Audrain County,* published in 1884, described the place Robinson and his wife had then occupied for eleven years. Most of the land was still in native grasses with 255 acres devoted to corn, oats and beans. There was a herd of 100 sheep as well as 30 milk cows and 100 beef cattle with two thoroughbred short-horn bulls.

When the book was written, Robinson had 38 horses on his property, two of these stallions. No doubt buyers sought animals they could say Robinson had selected or bred for smooth gait and quiet nature.

The horse barn, just one of many large outbuildings, included an indoor ring for winter work. The house was "handsome" according to the Audrain historian, filled with lovely furniture and art objects from all over the world. In days when running water was an extreme luxury, Robinson had it not only in the house but in the barns and paddocks, from a live well.

An earlier writer had written of Robinson's striking, pleasing physical appearance, and the historian heaped on him many coveted compliments of the time: "He is every inch a man; brave, generous, charitable and chivalrous to a fault, modest as a maiden . . . this prince of equestrians."

A few details about Robinson from interviews reprinted in the *Mexico Ledger* in 1957 from late 1880s issues:

He never really liked the circus. As soon as he could afford to, he traveled separately, slept and ate elsewhere. There was then quite a stigma on circus people and he felt it was somewhat deserved. He disliked particularly, the "stale jokes and vulgar wit" of clowns and said that the only good thing about the circus was the million dollars they'd paid him. Even this couldn't make him forget his broken bones.

When asked about the danger of his work, Robinson said that the worst injury he had ever had was a sprained neck that prevented his working for two years. "The principal thing in bareback riding," he said, "is to start and stop. That is where the power of balance is tested." He said his act required far less exertion than one might imagine, his two-a-day half-hour performances "merely good exercise."

When asked about his horses, Robinson discussed only one, his favorite, and he did not mention its name or say any more than that it was reliable. "I know him and he knows me. He knows what's expected of him and how to do it."

Materials about Robinson are sparse and none gives a full description of his act, which he changed from time to time. For the championship contest he was said to have entered the ring with "a personality of showmanship which indicated complete confidence." He first did some of the usual bareback feats, but with more grace and finish than others could muster. He did four-and-a-half-foot jumps in various postures on the horse; he rode through banners and balloons doing assorted gymnastics. A newspaper story said, "Like a graceful cat he was all over the horse's back then off, then on, then off, all with appearance of no effort." He also performed without saddle or pad, something no other rider had attempted up to that time.

As friends, Robinson sought out professional men. A younger relative said he obviously envied them their community status and settled lives, concluding, "Had he been reared in a normal manner and given a choice of careers, I'm sure he'd have been a journalist or an attorney."

The woman Robinson married, Laura Gorman, was refined and accomplished, a member of a prosperous and respected southern family. Though her brother had profitable business dealings with Robinson, the Gormans were aghast at the idea of their daughter marrying a circus performer. The only answer was to elope, and the marriage was described by a nephew as very happy, his wife always along when Robinson traveled.

No mention was made in these clippings of any children, but Robinson did add two young men to his act, possibly taking a mentor role with them. One dim, old newspaper picture shows him balanced on a horse's back on one foot, the other leg extended forward at right angles to his body. On his head is a smaller man, also balanced on one foot, opposite leg extended identically.

Robinson's death is listed as occurring in 1917 in French Lick, Indiana. He would have been 82 years old. No details are given as to why he was there. But whether or not he retained his Audrain property until the end, James Robinson put Missouri on the map as being the home of the world's champion bareback rider.

"a quick, convincing act of being a simple farmer who adored the Confederacy . . ."

James Rollins
Father of the University of Missouri

James Sidney Rollins is well remembered in the Columbia area by the title "Father of the University" because he was the man to introduce every legislation that had to do with establishing and equipping Missouri's first university. He also donated freely for its financial needs and served on its board of curators.

Rollins was involved with many important advancements in Boone County and throughout the state. He was partner with Middleton G. Singleton, Thomas January, and others in founding the town of Centralia and made at least two significant donations there, including several lots to be used for a factory and others to be used for a school.

Rollins was concerned with furthering educational opportunity for Missourians because he was convinced this was the only route to progress. He played a key role in establishing Columbia college, originally for women only, and as a legislator he wrote laws creating the School of Mines at Rolla and the Normal Schools in Kirksville and Warrensburg, now branches of the state university system.

But Rollins's interests didn't stop in the classroom. He was a leader among Missouri Whigs, served in both the state and the national legislatures, twice ran a close race for state governor, was almost a vice-presidential candidate, and wrote laws making it possible to establish the mental hospital in Fulton.

Many writers have speculated about how different Missouri's role in the Civil War might have been if Rollins had been governor. Although he held more slaves than anyone else in Boone County, Rollins believed in abolishing slavery and was opposed to the extension of slavery into new states. While strongly in favor of state's rights, he was equally concerned with preserving the Union.

As a native of Madison County, Kentucky, and the son of a wealthy doctor, Rollins was educated in law at Transylvania University in Lexington, and was intern to the legendary Boone County attorney, Abiel Leonard.

In Columbia, Rollins set up his own practice and married Mary E. Hickman, daughter of a prominent Columbia business and civic leader. Eleven children were born to this couple and Rollins's friends remembered with fond amusement how prone he was to find an excuse, in public speeches and private conversations, to discuss his family.

Rollins was an attentive and helpful friend and carried on voluminous correspondence with many people, most of whom were prominent in their time and some that turned out to be lastingly famous. He had a special close and longtime relationship with the Missouri artist George Caleb Bingham. Revering Bingham's talent, perhaps consciously hoping to prevent its being lost to the state, Rollins served as supporter and counselor through the many losses and discouragements of Bingham's life.

Outside of the political arena, Rollins must have had considerable physical courage, too, for he traveled often and widely as part of his assorted work and concerns. Some of his experiences show how hazardous this could be, especially just before and during the Civil War. Rollins was among the passengers in the stagecoach to St. Charles that was stopped and robbed in Centralia on September 27, 1864, the day guerrilla bands massacred a troop of Union soldiers commanded by A. V. E. Johnson. Legend and historians tell us Jesse and Frank James participated.

A wealthy man, Rollins made many donations for the betterment of his world. Professor W. B. Smith called him "First Citizen of the State."

John Crighton writes that Rollins did a quick, convincing act of being a simple farmer who adored the Confederacy. Centralia physician Achilles Sneed at once came to Rollins's aid, putting into his own pockets papers that would have told the outlaws they had a Unionist leader who would make a valuable hostage. Sneed then took Rollins to the attic of a business building where he was safe until the terrible day ended.

Another time, Rollins was captured by guerrillas looting Providence and was threatened with death, but some women appealed to the commanding officer's better impulses and he was spared. The public esteem Rollins enjoyed is demonstrated in still another incident: once Confederate forces pausing in Columbia confiscated the strong Unionist's fine horses. A party of Secessionist neighbors went to the rebel camp and negotiated most of the animals back to Rollins.

A different sort of adventure adds still more perspective on Rollins and his times. Once, when hired to defend a slave accused of rape, he found the crowd unwilling to wait for legal procedures. The first time they took the man out to lynch him, Rollins cut him down. The second time, Rollins, with the prominent newspaper editor W. F. Switzler at his side, was able to talk the crowd into leaving the man in jail. On the third try, they eluded Rollins and did kill the prisoner.

Injuries in a train wreck, not immediately recognized and treated, started a physical decline that took almost a decade to kill James S. Rollins. Though he fought to continue with causes that concerned him, Rollins died at 76 in 1888, after a year or so of partial paralysis. His life is remembered in several books, and in streets and buildings named after him in Columbia and elsewhere. A bronze bust of Rollins is displayed in Jesse Hall at the University of Missouri-Columbia. A wealthy man, he had made many donations for the betterment of his world. Some of these were recounted by W. B. Smith, a university professor of mathematics and astronomy, whose biography of Rollins appeared only three years after the death of the man he termed "First Citizen of the State."

“she was arrested . . . and is said to have flirted her way to escape”

Belle Starr
Outlaw Woman

The chivalrous traveler stopped at once for the beckoning well-dressed lady on the side of the road.

"My horse has gone lame," she said, "Could you help me?"

He dismounted and she descended from her sidesaddle into his arms, then from her skirts she drew a dainty little pistol and crisply told him to hand her his gun, take the saddle off her horse and put it on his own and to lead her animal to a certain blacksmith in the next town and leave it. His horse would be there waiting for him in a few days' time.

"You must be Belle Starr," the man said and she replied, smiling, from the back of his valuable animal, "I must be."

This is one of hundreds of stories of a Missourian who possibly has been the country's most-written-about woman. She has been featured in or had a prominent role in dozens of novels and movies and has been the topic of countless articles in varied publications, pamphlets and nonfiction books. Like the James Gang, she probably did only a fraction of what she's credited with, but it does appear that she knew some of the more famous outlaws very well. She seems to have been a woman far ahead of her time as to independence. No wonder the myths are hard to sort out.

Born Myra Maybelle Shirley in 1848 in Jasper County, near Carthage, Missouri, Belle Starr's background was not what we'd expect. Her father was a respected businessman whose property, including a hotel the family lived in and operated, dominated one side of the Carthage square. Myra was sent to the Carthage Female Academy where she did well even in such subjects as Greek, Latin and algebra, though music was her favorite. She was popular with her classmates, who considered her "nice and pretty," even if some of her blood came from the feuding Hatfields.

And from her brother Bud, whom she idolized, Belle gained not-so-girlish skills. He taught her to be a superb and fearless horsewoman, and a crack shot with all kinds of guns. This proved a blessing in her 15th year, when the Civil War was beginning to affect Missouri acutely. Belle rode her horse 40 miles cross country, jumping fences and ditches when necessary, to warn her guerilla brother that Union soldiers were advancing toward his group.

The following year Bud was killed and Belle rode with her father to Sarcoxie to claim his body. There she brandished guns and declared she would kill Union soldiers at every opportunity.

The Shirleys were among many Carthage people who had lost homes and livelihoods in the war. They moved to the Dallas, Texas, area. There, at the rather late age (for the time) of 19, Belle married another displaced Missourian, Jim Reed. Back in their home state, at Rich Hill, they had two children, Rosie Lee, born in 1868, and a boy two years later, named Eddie.

Reed, a former guerilla, chose after the war to ignore laws and it was not long before he had to take refuge, as many other bandits did, in Indian Territory. There Belle met Sam Starr, son of a Cherokee who gave them hospitality, but she went back to Dallas while her husband remained in hiding. She opened a gambling hall and was often seen with Cole Younger. This led to stories, possibly exaggerated, about their relationship and to the idea that Younger fathered Belle's daughter.

When Reed was arrested, Belle threatened to kill the deputy who did it and this man was later found dead. She apparently was not suspected; nobody was charged. Reed died in 1874, some say for the "dead or alive" reward on his head, others say killed by a lawman.

In 1876, Belle opened a livery stable near Dallas, seemingly to serve outlaw needs for good mounts and quick charges. She was arrested for fencing stolen horses and is said to have flirted her way to escape from the deputy. At some point, we're told, the infamous Indian Blue Duck, featured in the Larry McMurtry book and popular movie *Lonesome Dove,* was one of her loves. She also is said to have lived for some time with Bruce Younger, an uncle of the Younger brothers. During this period Belle's daughter, nicknamed Pearl, added Younger to her name.

In 1880, Belle married Sam Starr and they staked a large claim on the Canadian River in Oklahoma. Their ranch, called Younger's Bend, became an outlaw mecca. When arrested for horse theft and the possession of liquor, Belle and Starr were not appearing for their first time before Isaac C. Parker, "the hanging judge." He sentenced them each to a year in prison. They served less time than that, but when released returned to Younger's Bend and were soon in trouble again. Sam was killed in a shootout in 1886 or 1887 and Belle took another husband, Bill July, who changed his name to James July Starr. He was 15 years her junior, just a little older than her son, who left home in disgust.

Belle's principal biographer, Glenn Shirley, in *Belle Starr and Her Times,* says that, though a great deal of what's been written about her is untrue, the manner of her death is well documented. It came on a Sunday afternoon, February 3, 1889, just two days before her 41st birthday, when she was riding home from a friend's house. Someone knocked her off her horse with a shotgun blast from behind, then shot her in the face.

Reportedly, Pearl found her mother's body face down in the muddy road. Belle Starr was buried in the front yard of her home with Indian friends present following their custom of tossing pieces of cornbread onto the grave. The site was disturbed once, possibly for the pearl-handled revolvers buried with Belle. Pearl then had it elaborately covered with stone. A white marble marker is engraved with a picture of Belle's favorite horse, a bell and a star and a sentimental verse.

Belle Starr's birthplace can still be visited. It is a two-story white frame house outside Carthage on Highway 86, part of the reconstructed Ozarks town named Red Oak II. Admission to the village is free with a modest admission fee for touring the house, and there is an annual old-time music and dulcimer festival there in July every year.

“his congregation was 80, whose annual collections totaled a meager $100”

Augustine Tolton
Early African American Priest

Gus Tolton's life is a kind of Cinderella story. He left Missouri in 1861, at age seven, fleeing with his mother and three siblings through Ralls and Marion Counties to the banks of the mighty Mississippi. At the river's edge, a gang of Confederate sympathizers tried to stop the family from making like a banana (and splitting) into the Land of Lincoln and freedom. But federal troops intervened and secured them safe passage.

Tolton's mentors, the church authorities, gave him his first big break. With a flick of Fr. P. B. McGirr's wand, Tolton became a student in the all-white parish school at St. Peter's Church in Quincy, Illinois, upsetting segregationists and relieving Tolton of his toils as a stemmer at the Harris Tobacco Factory. Tolton tended the church furnace and studied his lessons, so impressing the German Franciscans with his virtue, intelligence and piety that they went to bat for him in Rome.

"If America has never seen a black priest, it has to see one now."

After five years of study in Rome's Eternal City, at the College of Propagation of the Faith, Tolton's prayers were answered. He was ordained to the priesthood in April 1886 in the Basilica of St. John Lateran. The million-dollar question was, Would Tolton, as a black man, be ordained for a foreign mission or a mission in Jim Crow America?

Challenging American noise about freedom and equality, Cardinal Simeoni put the matter to rest: "America has been called the most enlightened nation," he said. "We will see if it deserves that honor. If America has never seen a black priest, it has to see one now."

As it happened, the cardinal was blowing ritual smoke. In 1886, Tolton was assigned to manage a slapdash little outfit in the church's Negro Leagues. As pastor of St. Joseph's Catholic Church for Negroes, Tolton's congregation was 80, whose annual collections totaled a meager $100. Tolton was able to get away from his dead-end job by traveling to lecture and preach. Eventually he was transferred to Chicago, where he became pastor of St. Monica's Church for Negro Catholics, located in the city's slums. He died of apparent heat stroke coming home from a religious retreat.

"... a most fervent and pertinent speech in advocacy of the rights of his race ..."

James Milton Turner
A Great Black Orator

In September 1890, the *Indianapolis Freeman* asked its 7,000 readers to name the ten greatest African Americans in American history. When the ballots were counted, the results, by and large, were not surprising.

Most of the great instigators and agitators, the towering figures of 19th-century black revolt, had made the final cut. Frederick Douglass, Toussaint L'Ouverture, T. Thomas Fortune, James Milton Turner . . . James Milton who?

Turner's accomplishments as an educator, black rights advocate, diplomat and speaker were recognized at his death in 1915 by one of the largest funerals for a black person ever held in St. Louis. Thereafter, his contributions were largely forgotten.

"Few if any Negro leaders of his accomplishments have been less noted by historical writers than James Milton Turner, who was without question the most outstanding member of his race to be born and raised in Missouri," Dilliard wrote.

In 1934, historian Irving Dilliard, scrounging for rare morsels of biographical information on James Milton Turner, noted that his subject's reputation was all but buried with the man.

Turner was born a slave in St. Louis County, Missouri, in 1840. The few verifiable facts about his early years conflict with the only account he gave of his youth, which appeared in 1911 in a 4,000-word profile in the *St. Louis Post-Dispatch.*

Turner's bitterness, following a lifelong struggle for status and recognition, may have led him to embellish the story of how he was purchased out of slavery. According to Turner's version, his mother, Hannah, first appraised at $3,000, broke her hand; his father, a veterinarian, was able to persuade a doctor to diagnose the break as requiring amputation. Her price was then dropped to $400, a sum his father could afford, and James Milton was tossed into the deal for an extra $50.

Gary Kremer, Turner's most recent, most scholarly, and most thorough biographer, examined Hannah Turner's deed of emancipation and found no evidence to support the story of his purchase and other of Turner's recollections. "The 1911 interview with James Milton Turner is an intriguing reminiscence," he wrote. "It is also highly exaggerated, so much so that it invites skepticism on every point." What is clear is that Turner was born in a city and state that by the 1850s were divided over the question of slavery. Slaves in St. Louis tended to live in a less restrictive environment than their rural counterparts, and some worked in occupations permitting them to earn money and buy their freedom. Yet they nevertheless lived in a conservative state: In 1847, when Turner was eight, Missouri enacted a law making it a crime to provide a black person with a formal education, punishable by a $500 fine and up to six months in jail.

He was forced to "escape for his life at midnight, barefooted in the snow, leaving his shoes behind him."

Turner began to emerge as a political force in post-war Missouri politics, with a coming-out party in October 1865 at the organizational meeting of the Missouri Equal Rights League. There, the 26-year-old ex-slave made a speech characterized by the *Missouri Democrat* as "a most fervent and pertinent speech in advocacy of the rights of his race." Turner became secretary of the Missouri Equal Rights League and, at some personal risk, carried its message across the state. He spent much of his time in southeast Missouri, where rebel sympathies still ran high. At one point he was forced to "escape for his life at midnight, barefooted in the snow, leaving his shoes behind him."

Hired by the Kansas City school board, Turner spent 1868 teaching in the first black public school in the state; in 1869, he taught at a black school in Boonville, Missouri. He developed a reputation as a leading spokesman for black education in Missouri, and in 1869 the Federal Bureau of Refugees, Freedmen and Abandoned Lands hired Turner to investigate the condition of black schools in the state. In that capacity, Turner played a key role in expanding opportunities for Missouri blacks to obtain formal education.

Turner's political connections fostered his career. In March 1871 President Ulysses S. Grant named Turner minister to Liberia, making him the second black in U.S. history to be appointed to the country's diplomatic corps. Turner's stint in Liberia lasted seven years. When he returned to the United States in 1878, his attempts to resume his political career fizzled.

In 1879, Turner started the Colored Emigration Aid Association, an unsuccessful scheme to help resettle blacks in areas where their constitutional rights would be recognized and protected. He spent the final years of his life representing the former black slaves of the Cherokee in a legal dispute with the Cherokee tribe. At issue was the tribe's decision not to include their former slaves in the distribution of hundreds of thousands of federal dollars paid to the tribe in exchange for land. In 1888, after a long struggle, Turner's efforts paid off. Congress awarded $75,000 to the Cherokee, Shawnee and Delaware freedmen.

Turner also took an interest in the problems of the Choctaw and Chickasaw freedmen. While in Ardmore, Oklahoma, in September 1915, trying to collect fees for representing them, his right hand was cut by debris from the explosion of a nearby railroad car tank. The wound never healed, and Turner died from blood poisoning in November 1915.

**"an exclusive cure for baldness . . .
worked like fertilizer"**

C. J. Walker
Black Cosmetics Queen Millionaire

In a prophetic vision, an Afro-American male, lacking a barber's license but exceptionally savvy scalpwise, interrupted Madame C. J. Walker's beauty rest to let her in on an exclusive cure for baldness. Walker tried the formula on herself and friends and found it worked like fertilizer. She dumped Malone's Wonderful Hair Grower, an elixir she was selling in Colorado, and began traveling throughout the South, banging on doors to sell her own tried-and-true hair-care and beauty products.

In a few years, C. J. (then 37) and her second husband, Charles, marshaled a sales force numbering in the thousands, opened a school in Pittsburgh called the Lelia College for Walker Hair Culturists, created salons where their customers would be pampered, and expanded their business internationally to Jamaica, Cuba, Haiti, Costa Rica and the Panama Canal.

Walker's ads suggested the road to beauty and success was paved with her line of soaps, shampoos and powders. These toiletries, of unsurpassed quality, made Walker herself fabulously wealthy.

She had picked, scrubbed and washed her way out of childhood poverty on a Louisiana cotton plantation and out of wage slavery in St. Louis to become the first U.S. self-made woman millionaire. With her wealth, she built a beautiful house in New York on the Hudson River and lived in style. She also gave generously to black schools, orphanages, homes and causes such as the National Association for the Advancement of Colored People (NAACP) and the Young Men's Christian Association (YMCA).

Walker had to fight to win recognition from black leaders for her pioneering efforts and contributions to the black community. Unable to persuade Booker T. Washington to allow her to speak at the 1912 convention of the National Negro Business League, she interrupted the proceedings and spoke anyway. "I am a woman who came from the cotton fields of the South," she told the startled assemblage. "I was promoted from there to the washtub. Then I was promoted to the cook kitchen, and from there I promoted myself into the business of manufacturing hair goods and preparations . . . I have built my own factory on my own ground."

The next year, invited back to the convention, this time *to speak*, she urged African American women to assert their economic independence. "I want to say to every Negro woman present, don't sit down and wait for the opportunities to come. . . . Get up and make them!"

20 Question Quiz

(How much have you forgotten about Forgotten Missourians Who Made History?)

1. Who was president for a day?

2. What state has a town named after him?

3. Which two forgotten Missourians who made history in this book are related?

4. How did William Beaumont study gastric juices?

5. What natural area did John Colter first discover?

6. Who is the Mother of Kindergarten?

7. What did Jim the Wonder Dog do that was so amazing?

8. What is the last name of Hermann's biggest steamboating family?

9. Who founded Missouri's most successful commune?

10. Who was famous for smashing kegs to abolish drinking?

11. Augustine Tolton was America's first ________.

12. Name two trails that Merrill Mattes wrote about.

13. Which writer's career began with the *Monkey Nest Monitor?*

14. Hannah Cole settled near which present-day city?

15. Who is Missouri's Father of Journalism?

16. Why was Pearl Curran not an ordinary housewife?

17. Charles Valentine Riley discovered the predator of the Cottony Cushion Scale in which country?

18. Whose hair care products worked like fertilizer and made her a millionaire?

19. Which Boone played ragtime piano?

20. Which Boone had 14 kids?

EXTRA POINT: Why did Gottfried Duden think the Missouri River Valley was so great? Do you agree?

See the last page in the book for clues!

ACKNOWLEDGMENTS

The Artley profile is reprinted in part with permission from Marlys Johnson, "See Dick and Jane and Spot and Dr. Artley," *Columbia Senior Times,* April 1996, Parry Publishing, Columbia, Mo. The Mattes profile is reprinted with permission from the *Kansas City Star,* May 7, 1996.

BIBLIOGRAPHY

Bills, Carole. *Nathan Boone, the forgotten hero.* Carole Bills, P. O. Box 15, Ash Grove, Mo., 1984.

Bradbury, John. *Travels in the Interior of America.* Liverpool, England, 1817.

Collins, A. Loyd, and Georgia I. Collins. *Hero Stories from Missouri History.* Kansas City, Mo.: Burton Publishing Company, 1956.

Commire, Anne. *Something about the Author*. Detroit, Mich.: Gale Research Book Tower, 1980.

Concise Dictionary of American Biography. 4th ed. Charles Scribner's Sons, n.d.

Conroy, Jack. "Memories of Arna Bontemps: Friend and Collaborator." *American Library,* December 1974.

Conroy, Jack. "On *Anvil.*" *TriQuarterly 43*, fall 1978.

Crighton, John. *The History of Columbia and Boone County*. Columbia, Mo.: Boone County Historical Society, 1987.

Dains, Mary K., ed. *Show Me Missouri Women: Selected Biographies.* Missouri Women's Historical Project, sponsored by the Missouri Division of the American Association of University Women. Kirksville, Mo.: Thomas Jefferson University Press, 1989.

Dictionary of American Biography. New York: Charles Scribner's Sons, 1946-1950.

Dilliard, Irving. "James Milton Turner: A Little Known Benefactor of His People." *Journal of Negro History,* October 1934.

Downey, Bill. *Tom Bass: Black Horseman.* St. Louis, Mo.: Saddle and Bridle Inc., 1975.

Dyer, Robert. *Big Canoe Songbook: Ballads from the Heartland.* Boonville, Mo.: Pekitanoui Publications, 1991.

Finck, Henry T. *My Adventures in the Golden Age of Music*. New York: Funk and Wagnells, 1926.

Foner, Philip S., and Sally M. Miller, eds. *Kate Richards O'Hare: Selected Writings and Speeches.* Baton Rouge: Louisiana State University Press, 1982.

Fried, Lewis. "Conversation with Jack Conroy." *New Letters,* fall 1972.

Hine, Darlene Clark, ed. *Black Women in America: An Historical Encyclopedia*. Brooklyn, N.Y.: Carlson Publishing Inc., 1993.

The History of Audrain County. Audrain Historical Society, Mexico, Missouri.

Horsman, Reginald. *Frontier Doctor: William Beaumont, America's First Great Medical Scientist.* Columbia, Mo.: University of Missouri Press, 1995.

James, Edward T., ed. *Notable American Woman, 1607-1950: A Biographical Dictionary* Cambridge, Mass.: Belknap Press, Harvard University Press, 1971.

Johnson, Rossiter. *The Twentieth Century Biographical Dictionary of Notable Americans.* Boston, Mass.: The Biographical Society, 1904.

Kremer, Gary R. *James Milton Turner and the Promise of America: The Public Life of a Post-Civil War Black Leader.* Columbia, Mo.: University of Missouri Press, 1991.

Logan, Rayford W., and Michael R. Winston. *Dictionary of American Negro Biography.* New York: W. W. Norton, n.d.

Meiners, Edwin P. "Charles Valentine Riley." C. V. Riley Entomological Society, University of Missouri, Columbia, Mo.

Missouri Biographical Dictionary: People of All Times and Places Who Have Been Important to the History and Life of the State. New York: Somerset Publishers Inc., 1995.

Missouri Folklore Society Journal. Missouri Folklore Society, Columbia, Mo.

Missouri Historical Review. Missouri Historical Society, Columbia, Mo.

Mitchell, Clarence Dewey. *Jim, the Wonder Dog.* Red Cross Pharmacy, Marshall, Mo., 1983.

Nation, Carry A. *The Use and Need of the Life of Carry A. Nation. Written by Herself.* Alpena Pass, Arkansas.

Nordhoff, Charles. *The Communistic Societies of the United States.* Corner House, 1978.

Pfening, Fred. "William Preston Hall." *Missouri Historical Review,* 1968.

Shirley, Glenn. *Belle Starr and Her Times: The Literature, the Facts, and the Legends.* University of Oklahoma Press, 1990.

Shoemaker, Floyd Calvin. *Missouri's Hall of Fame: Lives of Eminent Missourians.* Columbia, Mo.: Missouri Book Company, 1923.

Thompson, Robert. "An Interview with Jack Conroy." *Missouri Review,* fall 1983.

Warfel, Harry R. *American Novelists of Today*. New York: American Book Company, 1951.

Wilson, Suzanne. "The Lady Was a Caver." *Missouri Conservationist,* March 1993.

Wixson, Douglas. *Worker-Writer in America: Jack Conroy and the Tradition of Midwestern Literary Radicalism, 1898-1990*. Chicago: University of Illinois Press, 1994.

About the authors

This book was a cooperative effort by seven Missouri authors interested in bringing little-known Missouri heritage to the light of interested readers. Look for their other books for more reading on what made our state great.

Jim Borwick

Jim Borwick has worked at newspapers in South Carolina, Idaho, New York and Missouri, including the *Island Packet* in Hilton Head, South Carolina, the *Wood River Journal* in Idaho, the *River Reporter* in New York and the *River Valley Review* in Missouri.

Jim was born and raised in Monticello, New York. He went to Kenyon College in Gambier, Ohio, where he studied history. He received his law degree from the University of Idaho College of Law.

He currently resides in Columbia, Missouri, where he is an electronic resource assistant at the University of Missouri-Columbia's Ellis Library. He also works at MU's law library.

In his spare time, he likes to "ditz around on the guitar and eat."

Brett Dufur

Brett Dufur is the author of *The Complete Katy Trail Guidebook* and *Best of Missouri Hands: Profiles of the State's Fine Artists and Craftsmen.*

He is also the founder, editor and publisher of Pebble Publishing, a publishing house of regional interest books in Rocheport, Missouri.

He is currently working on a nature guide to the Missouri River Valley; a book entitled *The River Revisited*, documenting the 1996 Lewis and Clark keelboat reenactment comparing the river in 1804 to the present; and also a guide to another favorite Missouri topic: *Exploring Missouri Wine Country*.

He has worked at *Costa Rica Guide* magazine, *Missouri Magazine* and at several newspapers in Arkansas and Missouri, as well as *Constructor de Caminos*, a Latin American trade magazine. He also does freelance photography and writing.

Brett was born and raised in Kansas City, Missouri. He received both his journalism degree and a degree in Latin American Studies from the University of Missouri-Columbia.

He spends his off hours getting tangled up in words, traveling and exploring with his dog Daisy.

Joan Gilbert

Joan Gilbert most recently authored a University of Missouri release titled *Trail of Tears across Missouri,* which is part of the Missouri Heritage Readers series. She has also written *House of Whispers* in 1972, which was published by Paperback Library, now a part of Warners Media Group, and *Summerhill Summer* by Bethany Press in 1968.

In addition to books, Joan has written some 600 pieces of short fiction on horses, Missouri history and country living for magazines such as *Small Farm* and *Back Home*.

Her writing has won her 20 awards from organizations including the Missouri Writers Guild, Missouri Press Women, and the National Federation of Press Women. These awards include a prize from the James Younger Gang based in St. Joseph and a first prize from the Ozark Writers League.

Joan was born and grew up in Dixon, Missouri, and received her B.S. in Secondary Education in Springfield, Missouri. Today, she lives near Hallsville, where she continues writing books and articles, including a book on Missouri ghost sightings, to be published by Pebble Publishing.

Margot Ford McMillen

Margot Ford McMillen's most recent book, *A to Z Missouri: The Dictionary of Missouri Place Names*, was published by Pebble Publishing in 1996. In 1995, she was invited by the Secretary of State Rebecca Cook to write the keynote essay on childhood for the *Missouri Blue Book*, the state manual. In 1994, the University of Missouri Press published her book *Paris, Tightwad, and Peculiar: Missouri Place Names* as part of its Missouri Heritage Readers series.

Margot is also a regular contributor to the *Missouri Conservationist*. From 1988 to 1994, she published *Our Missouri*, a quarterly journal for elementary students studying Missouri history and culture. McMillen's book *The Masters and Their Traditional Arts* and a series of brochures on Missouri traditions were published by the Missouri Cultural Heritage Center at the University of Missouri-Columbia in 1986.

Margot's earliest articles appeared in the St. Louis and Kansas City newspapers, and since then she has written for national quilting magazines, farming magazines and old-time music magazines. She received her B.A. from Northwestern University in Evanston, Illinois, and her M.A. in English from the University of Missouri-Columbia.

Margot was born and raised in Chicago and she moved to Missouri in 1972. She has lived in Missouri ever since, and has raised two daughters in

Callaway County. She teaches critical thinking for the English Department at Westminster College in Fulton and lives on a farm in Callaway County. There she has devoted herself to learning and writing about the folklife of the state. She is married to Professor Howard Marshall of the University of Missouri-Columbia Department of Art and Archaeology. On their farm, they raise Salers cattle and enjoy a varying selection of dogs, cats, horses, hogs and chickens.

Dorothy Heckmann Shrader

Shrader is author of *Steamboat Legacy: The Life and Times of a Steamboat Family.* She recently finished a book entitled *Steamboat Treasures, The Inadvertent Biography of a Steamboat Man*. Both were published by the Wein Press, of Hermann, Missouri.

Shrader received two degrees from the University of Missouri-Columbia — one in journalism in 1935 and one in education in 1947. Graduate study in Iowa led to work in special education. She was principal of Wilson School for the Educably Retarded and founder of the Beloit Campus School for the Emotionally Disturbed in Ames. At the same time, she ran her own small publishing business, editing and publishing *The Bulletin Board: A Guide to Ames* for 25 years and serving as the city's public relations officer. In retirement, she has devoted her time to researching Missouri River history.

Dorothy Heckmann Shrader was born in Hermann, Missouri. She attended school in Hermann and spent her summers living and working with her parents aboard the steamer *John Heckmann.*

Dr. William Shrader, her husband of 58 years, is an Iowa State University emeritus professor of agronomy.

William Taft

For more than 35 years, Dr. William H. Taft taught journalism, the last 25 years at the University of Missouri-Columbia. His special research concerned Missouri newspapers, and he has written three books on this topic.

His most recent book, *Wit & Wisdom of Missouri's Country Editors*, published by Pebble Publishing, highlights pithy phrases and quotes from Missouri's papers of the past.

Previous books by Taft include *Missouri Newspapers* (University of Missouri Press, 1964); *Missouri Newspapers: When and Where, 1808-1963,* a listing of more than 6,000 newspapers that have appeared in the state (State Historical Society of Missouri, 1964); *Newspapers as Tools for Historians* (Lucas Brothers, 1967); *American Magazines for the 1980s* (Hastings House, New York, 1982); *Encyclopedia of Twentieth-Century Journalists* (Garland, New York, 1986); *Missouri Newspapers and the Missouri Press Association: 125 Years of Service, 1867-1992* (Heritage House, 1992). He has also published numerous encyclopedia articles, *Journalism Quarterly* articles and others.

Dr. Taft was born in Mexico, Missouri. He began his newspaper career as a teenager on the *Mexico Ledger*, writing "locals" and a high school column. At Westminster he handled public relations. He received degrees from Westminster College, University of Missouri and the Western Reserve University. He has taught at Youngston, Hiram and Defiance Colleges in Ohio, and founded the journalism program at Memphis State University prior to returning to Columbia in 1956. He retired in 1981 as Professor Emeritus from the University of Missouri-Columbia Journalism School and continues as historian of the Missouri Press Association and remains involved in other research projects.

He has been married for more than 55 years to his wife, Myrtle, and they have three children.

Pamela Watson

For 17 years, Pamela Watson has written travel articles, sports and features for *PC Magazine, Reader's Digest* and *Private Clubs Magazine*, as well as numerous newspapers and regional publications.

She is also the author of *99 Fun Things to Do in Columbia and Boone County*, published by Pebble Publishing.

Her interests include history and exploring the backroads of Missouri, both for adventure and as a subtle way of teaching history to her children.

The fiery life of illustrator Joe Fox

Joe Fox presently lives in Idaho, where he is a smokejumper and freelance artist. Smokejumpers are a die-hard crew of forest firefighters in the West who jump from planes and parachute into rugged, remote hot spots deep in the wilderness not easily reached by road to put out and redirect the rampant spread of wild fires.

In fact, the progress of this book's creation was paced by the West's fires more than any publishing schedule. A typical conversation as this book progressed was Joe calling in saying, "The fires are subsiding a bit so I think I'll be able to get back to drawing soon."

Brett Dufur, the editor on the project, recalls the late night calls from Joe as *Forgotten Missourians Who Made History* took shape.

"Joe was basically living out of hotel rooms all over Utah and Idaho as his crew followed the rampaging fires. He'd call in for direction and inspiration on the project very, very late at night," Brett said. "We really wanted Joe to do the work, so we just waited by the phone for him to call and tell us the fires were starting to taper off a bit."

Joe's very diverse talents and interests keep him busy but balanced.

"I like the variety of my work. I was working outdoors all fall season fighting forest fires, so it's nice to get back to illustrating. My work days and my idea of 'vacation' are the complete opposite of most peoples. I spend my work days out in the forest and then look forward to sitting down indoors to create new drawings as my escape."

His cartoon-style illustrations are a result of the same techniques used by newspaper comic strippers. Artists do a line drawing and then cut and place sheets of small dots of varying densities onto the drawings to create the varying shades of greys and blacks. Look closely at Joe's illustrations and then at the comic section of your Sunday newspaper, and you will see this technique.

Joe has a degree in law from the University of Idaho College of Law, a Ph.D. in entomology from the University of California-Berkeley, an M.A. in zoology from the University of California-Davis, and a B.S. in biology from the University of San Francisco.

Joe Fox was born in North Carolina and grew up in California. His mother's family has roots in Miller County, Missouri, and property beneath the Bagnell Dam reservoir. One of her relatives has the distinction of having been hanged by Quantrell's Raiders. Joe's great, great grandmother on his father's side was born in Missouri in 1848.

Index

The Show Me Missouri Series

99 Fun Things to Do in Columbia & Boone County

ISBN: 0-9646625-2-3

Guide to 99 hidden highlights, unique dining, galleries, museums, towns, people and history in Columbia, Rocheport, Centralia and Boone County. Most trips are free or under $10. Includes maps, photos, accessibility of sites. Fully indexed. 168 pages. By Pamela Watson. $12.95

A to Z Missouri

ISBN: 0-9646625-4-X

Abo to Zwanzig! A dictionary-style book of Missouri place name origins. Includes history for each town and community, pronunciations, population, county, post office dates and more. 220 pages. By Margot Ford McMillen. $14.95

Best of Missouri Hands

ISBN: 0-9646625-5-8

Profiles of Missouri's fine artists and craftsmen. From porcelain to wood and pewter to gold, *Best of Missouri Hands* shows the best our state has to offer. This book highlights many traditional art forms and techniques, and the artists behind the expressions. 152 pages. By Brett Dufur. $12.95

Daytrip Missouri

ISBN: 0-9651340-0-8

Information on tourist attractions throughout the state. Topics include history, up-to-date attraction information, a listing of annual events and helpful travel tips for more than 40 locations around the state, and travel notes by Missouri tourism directors. In addition, 60 black and white photos and 20 maps make this the tour guide standard for Missouri. 224 pages. By Lee N. Godley and Patricia Murphy O'Rourke. $14.95

Exploring Missouri Wine Country

ISBN: 0-9646625-6-6

This guidebook to Missouri Wine Country offers an intimate look at Missouri's winemakers and wineries, including how to get there, their histories and the story of how Missouri came to have its own Rhineland. Includes wine tips, recipes, home-brew recipes, dictionary of wine terms and more. Also lists nearby Bed and Breakfasts and lodging. 168 pages. By Brett Dufur. $14.95

Forgotten Missourians Who Made History

ISBN: 0-9646625-8-2

A book of short stories and humorous comic-style illustrations of more than 35 Missourians who made a contribution to the state or nation yet are largely forgotten by subsequent generations. By Jim Borwick and Brett Dufur. $14.95

The Complete Katy Trail Guidebook

ISBN: 0-9646625-0-7

The most complete guide to services, towns, people, places and history along Missouri's 200-mile Katy Trail. This updated edition covers the cross-state hiking and biking trail from Clinton to St. Charles — now America's longest rails-to-trails project. Includes trailhead maps, 80 photos, Flood of '93, how to make blueberry wine, uses for Missouri mud and more. 168 pages. By Brett Dufur. $14.95

What's That?

ISBN: 0-9646625-1-5

A Nature Guide to the Missouri River Valley

Companion guide to the *Katy Trail Guidebook.* This easy-to-use, illustrated four-season guide identifies trees, flowers, birds, animals, insects, rocks, fossils, clouds, reptiles, footprints and more. Features the Missouri River Valley's most outstanding sites and nature daytrips. 176 pages. Compiled by Brett Dufur. $14.95

Wit & Wisdom

ISBN: 0-9646625-3-1

of Missouri's Country Editors

A compilation of over 600 pithy sayings from pioneer Missouri newspapers. Many of these quotes and quips date to the 19th century yet remain timely for today's readers. Richly illustrated and fully indexed to help you find that perfect quote. 168 pages. By William Taft. $14.95

Pebble Publishing

P.O. Box 431 ❖ Columbia, MO 65205-0431

(800) 576-7322 ❖ Fax: (573) 698-3108

Quantity	*Book Title*	*x Unit Price =*	*Total*

Mo. residents add 6.975% sales tax =-----------

Shipping ($1.24 each book) x =-----------

Total =-----------

Name:______________________________

Address:___________________ Apt.______

City, State, Zip_______________________

Phone: (____) ______________________

Credit Card # __________________________

Expiration Date _____/_____/_____ Please send catalog _____

Visit ***Trailside Books*** online at http://www.trailsidebooks.com

Show Me Missouri books are available at many local bookstores. They can also be ordered directly from the publisher, using this form, or ordered by phone, fax or over the Internet.

Pebble Publishing also distributes 100 other books of regional interest, rails-to-trails, Missouri history, heritage, nature, recreation and more. These are available through our online bookstore and mail-order catalog. Visit our online bookstore, called ***Trailside Books*** at http://www.trailsidebooks.com, or leave a message at brett@trailsidebooks.com. If you would like to receive our catalog, please fill out and mail the form on the previous page.

Clues for 20 Question Quiz on pages 130-131.

1. See page 7.
2. See page 7.
3. See page 101 & 103.
4. See page 13.
5. See page 37.
6. See page 17.
7. See page 81.
8. See page 73.
9. See page 83.
10. See page 97.
11. See page 123.
12. See page 95.
13. See page 43.
14. See page 31.
15. See page 27.
16. See page 51.
17. See page 107.
18. See page 129.
19. See page 19.
20. See page 25.